Wagohan : The ABCs of Japanese Cuisine

和ごはん101

山田玲子
Reiko Yamada

ポット出版

はじめに

　和食は、2013年にユネスコ無形文化遺産に登録され、以前にも増して世界から熱い視線が注がれています。最近は、世界の多くの街で、ラーメン店、居酒屋、おにぎりの店などが増え、庶民の定番メニューも大人気になっているようです。そこであらためて、和食って何？と考えてみたくなったのがこの本を作るきっかけとなりました。

　私が最初に和食を意識したのは、30年前に交換ホームステイでオーストラリアの主婦が我が家にやってきた時です。彼女は朝晩のなんでもない日常の食事に、「なんてきれいで、ヘルシーな食事なの！」と感動し、外食で蕎麦を食べれば、ざるから小皿の薬味にまで興味津々でした。その後、私は料理を教えはじめるようになり、早20年。その間海外での料理イベントやクラスで、巻き寿司のデモンストレーションを行なったり、屋台の焼きそばなどを紹介したところ、大好評でした。和食の幅の広さと魅力に私自身も新たな発見をし、食は身近な外交で、国際交流の最大のツールだと確信しました。

　和食という言葉は、1920年代にはじめて国語辞典に登場したそうです。洋食が入ってきたことで、和食の特徴が浮かび上がったということかもしれません。発酵食品やだしなどの旨み成分の独特な味、四季を尊び、楽しむという伝統と豊かな感受性が和食に反映されていると思います。

　この本では、日常の和食を中心とした普段着の食文化を紹介したいと思い、受け継がれている伝統行事や食材の歴史や由来、道具なども含めて、身近にある食卓まわりをまとめてみました。異文化コミュニケーションのツールの一つとして、お役に立てれば幸いです。

山田玲子

Introduction

With Japanese food, or "washoku," added to UNESCO's Intangible Cultural Heritage list in 2013, it's drawing more international attention now than ever before. In cities across the globe, rustic staples like ramen, onigiri, or izakaya dishes are gaining popularity. But what really is Japanese food? I decided to write this book to revisit that question.

The first time I started to appreciate Japanese food was 30 years ago, when an Australian woman visited my house for a homestay program. She would exclaim how beautiful and healthy the meal was when served my ordinary no-frills breakfast. Dining at a soba restaurant, she admired everything from the sieve to the small plates of condiments and toppings. And now, after 20 years as a cooking adviser, I've hosted various events and classes across the world, filled with people eager to learn about food stall yakisoba or the perfect sushi roll. Through these experiences I have rediscovered the versatility and beauty of Japanese cuisine and firmly believe food to be the greatest tool for fostering cross-cultural understanding.

Tracing its roots, I learned that the word "washoku" was added to the Japanese dictionary in the 1920s. Perhaps the introduction of Western food spurred the necessity to define the characteristics of Japanese food. From the range of fermented products to the umami flavor in dashi stock, this cuisine reflects our unique tradition and rich sensibility of honoring the four seasons.

Here I introduce the everyday dishes of Japanese food culture, also touching upon annual traditions and the history of commonly used ingredients and tools. It's my hope that this book will come in handy as another resource to communicate with people across nations and cultures.

Reiko Yamada

目次

はじめに ……… 2

基本の朝ごはん

001：ごはん ……… 12
002：味噌汁 ……… 14
003：焼き魚 ……… 16
004：おひたし ……… 16
005：漬物 ……… 17
006：納豆 ……… 17
007：だし巻き卵 ……… 18

定番ごはん

008：卵かけごはん ……… 24
009：茶漬け ……… 24
010：炊き込みごはん ……… 25
011：赤飯 ……… 25
012：そうめん ……… 26
013：蕎麦 ……… 26
014：うどん ……… 26
015：冷やし中華 ……… 28
016：ラーメン ……… 28
017：焼きそば ……… 28
018：天丼 ……… 30
019：カツ丼 ……… 30
020：牛丼 ……… 31
021：親子丼 ……… 31
022：お好み焼き ……… 32
023：たこ焼き ……… 32
024：お弁当 ……… 34
025：おにぎり ……… 35

人気の一品

026：ハンバーグ ……… 40
027：生姜焼き ……… 40

028：ナポリタン ……… 40
029：カレーライス ……… 41
030：餃子 ……… 42
031：肉じゃが ……… 42
032：コロッケ ……… 43
033：から揚げ ……… 43
034：金目の煮付け ……… 44
035：鯖味噌 ……… 44
036：ぶりの照り焼き ……… 45
037：刺身 ……… 45
038：きんぴらごぼう ……… 46
039：胡麻和え ……… 46
040：ポテトサラダ ……… 47
041：鶏の照り焼き ……… 47
042：焼き鳥 ……… 48
043：枝豆 ……… 48
044：山かけ ……… 49
045：冷奴 ……… 49
046：総菜パン ……… 50
047：中華まん ……… 52

ごちそうごはん

048：手巻き寿司 ……… 58
049：天ぷら ……… 59
050：すき焼き ……… 60
051：寄せ鍋 ……… 61
052：しゃぶしゃぶ ……… 62
053：おでん ……… 64

季節のごはん

054：お節 ……… 72
055：餅 ……… 74
056：雑煮 ……… 75
057：福豆 ……… 77
058：恵方巻き ……… 77
059：ちらし寿司 ……… 79

本書の特徴は、日本文は日本人の読者に、英文は外国人の読者に向けて、内容を変えているところがあります。
その違いも合わせてお楽しみください。

060：潮汁 ……… 79
061：桜餅 ……… 79
062：三色団子 ……… 81
063：巻き寿司 ……… 81
064：いなり寿司 ……… 81
065：柏餅 ……… 83
066：ちまき ……… 83
067：筍ごはん ……… 83
068：鰻重 ……… 84
069：おはぎ ……… 86
070：月見団子 ……… 88
071：年越し蕎麦 ……… 90

いつもの飲みもの

072：日本茶 ……… 94
073：抹茶 ……… 96
074：日本酒 ……… 98
075：焼酎 ……… 99
076：ビール ……… 100
077：酎ハイ ……… 100
078：ワイン ……… 101
079：梅酒 ……… 101

和のお菓子

080：生菓子 ……… 104
081：あんみつ ……… 106
082：汁粉 ……… 106
083：ぜんざい ……… 106
084：どら焼き ……… 108
085：たい焼き ……… 109
086：かき氷 ……… 109
087：干菓子 ……… 110
088：わらび餅 ……… 112
089：くずきり ……… 112
090：ところてん ……… 113

和の材

091：醤油 ……… 116
092：みりん ……… 118
093：料理酒 ……… 118
094：胡麻油 ……… 120
095：ソース ……… 121
096：味噌 ……… 122
097：だし ……… 124
098：乾物 ……… 126
099：海藻 ……… 128
100：香辛料 ……… 130
101：和のハーブ ……… 132

和の道具

まな板と包丁 ……… 136
鍋類 ……… 138
竹の道具 ……… 140
木の道具 ……… 142
金物・瀬戸物道具 ……… 144

コラム：
一汁三菜の配膳 ……… 146
正しい箸のあつかい方 ……… 148
和の器 ……… 150
スーパーで買える日本のおみやげ ……… 152

レシピ ……… 154
プロフィール ……… 159

CONTENTS

Introduction ········ 3

The Basics of Breakfast

001 : Rice ········ 12
002 : Miso Soup ········ 14
003 : Grilled Fish ········ 16
004 : Boiled Vegetable ········ 16
005 : Pickles ········ 17
006 : Fermented Soy Beans ········ 17
007 : Japanese Rolled Omelet ········ 18

Staple Dishes

008 : Egg Raw over Rice ········ 24
009 : Soup over Rice ········ 24
010 : Mixed Rice ········ 25
011 : Red Bean Rice ········ 25
012 : Somen ········ 26
013 : Buckwheat Noodles ········ 26
014 : Thick Wheat Noodles ········ 26
015 : Cold Ramen ········ 28
016 : Ramen ········ 28
017 : Stir Fried Noodles ········ 28
018 : Tempura Bowl ········ 30
019 : Pork Cutlet Bowl ········ 30
020 : Beef Bowl ········ 31
021 : Chicken and Egg Bowl ········ 31
022 : Japanese Savory Pancake ········ 32
023 : Octopus Balls ········ 32
024 : Lunch Box ········ 34
025 : Rice Ball ········ 35

Popular Meals

026 : Japanese Salisbury Steak ········ 40
027 : Ginger Pork ········ 40

028 : Spaghetti Napolitana ········ 40
029 : Curry Rice ········ 41
030 : Pan Fried Dumplings ········ 42
031 : Meat and Potato Stew ········ 42
032 : Croquette ········ 43
033 : Japanese Fried Chicken ········ 43
034 : Braised Alfonsino ········ 44
035 : Mackerel Braised in Miso ········ 44
036 : Yellowtail Teriyaki ········ 45
037 : Sashimi ········ 45
038 : Braised Burdock Root and Carrot ········ 46
039 : Spinach with Sesame Sauce ········ 46
040 : Potato Salad ········ 47
041 : Chicken Teriyaki ········ 47
042 : Chicken Skewers ········ 48
043 : Edamame ········ 48
044 : Tuna with Grated Yam ········ 49
045 : Chilled Tofu ········ 49
046 : Bread Meals ········ 50
047 : Chinese Steamed Buns ········ 52

Festive Meals

048 : Hand-Rolled Sushi ········ 58
049 : Tempura ········ 59
050 : Sukiyaki ········ 60
051 : Mixed Hot Pot ········ 61
052 : Shabu-shabu ········ 62
053 : Oden ········ 64

Seasonal Dishes

054 : Festive Dishes for the New Year ········ 72
055 : Rice Cake ········ 74
056 : Rice Cake and Vegetables Soup ········ 75
057 : Fukumame ········ 77
058 : Eho-maki ········ 77
059 : Scattered Topping Sushi ········ 79

This book's content slightly differs between the Japanese and English text to best suit each reader.

060 : Clear Clam Soup ········ 79
061 : Mochi with Cherry Leaves ········ 79
062 : Tricolor Rice Dumplings ········ 81
063 : Rolled Sushi ········ 81
064 : Sushi Wrapped in Fried Tofu ········ 81
065 : Kashiwa Mochi ········ 83
066 : Chimaki ········ 83
067 : Bamboo Rice ········ 83
068 : Una-ju ········ 84
069 : Ohagi ········ 86
070 : Full Moon Rice Dumplings ········ 88
071 : Toshikosi Soba ········ 90

Everyday Drinks

072 : Japanese Tea ········ 94
073 : Matcha ········ 96
074 : Japanese Sake ········ 98
075 : Shochu ········ 99
076 : Beer ········ 100
077 : Chuhai ········ 100
078 : Wine ········ 101
079 : Plum Sake ········ 101

Japanese Sweets

080 : Fresh Japanese Confections ········ 104
081 : Anmitsu ········ 106
082 : Shiruko ········ 106
083 : Zenzai ········ 106
084 : Red Bean Pancake ········ 108
085 : Taiyaki ········ 109
086 : Kakigori ········ 109
087 : Dry Confections ········ 110
088 : Warabi Mochi ········ 112
089 : Kuzukiri ········ 112
090 : Tokoroten ········ 113

Japanese Ingredients

091 : Soy Sauce ········ 116
092 : Sweet Sake ········ 118
093 : Japanese Cooking Sake ········ 118
094 : Sesame Oil ········ 120
095 : Sauce ········ 121
096 : Fermented Soybean Paste ········ 122
097 : Dashi Stock ········ 124
098 : Dried Food ········ 126
099 : Seaweed ········ 128
100 : Japanese Spices ········ 130
101 : Japanese Herbs ········ 132

Japanese Tools

Cutting Board & Knife ········ 136
Pots ········ 138
Bamboo Wood Tools ········ 140
Wooden Tools ········ 142
Hardware and Pottery Goods ········ 144

COLUMNS :

Setting up the Table for Ichiju-Sansai with Japanese Tableware········ 146

Back to the Basics: How to Use Chopsticks ········ 148

Japanese Pottery ········ 150

Japanese Souvenirs Available at the Supermarket ········ 152

RECIPES ········ 154
PROFILE ········ 159

基本の朝ごはん
The Basics of Breakfast

When thinking of Japanese food, white rice and miso soup may first come to mind. Although fewer people eat Japanese style breakfast now, waking up in the morning to the aroma of dashi stock stimulates the traditional Japanese senses. The basic menu of ichiju-sansai, or one soup and three dishes, creates a healthy, nutritious, and ideal meal containing protein, minerals, and vitamins. Starting off the morning with this breakfast will surely boost your whole day.

和食といって、まず私が一番最初に思い浮かべるのは白いごはんとお味噌汁。
だしの香りで目覚める朝は、じわっと日本人のDNAが刺激され、
元気いっぱいな一日をスタートできます。
和食の基本「一汁三菜」は、タンパク質、ミネラル、ビタミンなど
栄養バランスのいい健康的なごはん。でも朝は忙しいもの。
まずは、肩の力を抜いて一汁一菜からスタートしてみるのもいいですね。

| 基本の朝ごはん | The Basics of Breakfast

001 ごはん
Gohan

美味しいお米は、今や沖縄から北海道まで日本全国で作られるようになり、ブランド米がたくさん登場。気候や風土、水などにより、味も香りも粘り気も違います。新米の時期も南から北上して6月下旬～11月上旬までと長くなり、いろいろな新米を食べ比べて楽しんでいます。私は、お米はもっぱら鍋で炊きます。炊飯時間も短く、お米が立って甘みがふくよか。お焦げもおまけの楽しみの一つです。

Rice: From Okinawa to Hokkaido, delicious rice is produced throughout Japan, with many brand-name rice appearing on the market. Since each region's climate, environment, and water differ from north to south, the taste, smell, and consistency of the rice will vary. Another characteristic of Japanese rice comes from the season in which it's harvested-from, late June to early November moving up north. Comparing and trying out different types of new rice is a fun way to take advantage of this. Even with cooking the rice, the flavor transforms just by using a clay pot or a pan instead of a rice cooker. Don't forget to savor the scorched rice.

いろいろな米 Various Types of Rice

白米
Hakumai
玄米を精米して胚芽をとった米。ふっくらモチモチとした食感で一番日本で食されている。
White Rice: This rice made by polishing brown rice and removing the germ has a fluffy and chewy texture and is the most popular type of rice in Japan.

玄米
Genmai
精白されないので、ビタミン、ミネラル、食物繊維の栄養素が豊富。
Brown Rice: Since this rice is unpolished, brown rice contains plenty of nutrients including vitamins, minerals, and dietary fiber.

雑穀米
Zakkokumai
黒米、大麦、粟、稗など数十種類の雑穀がある。不足しがちな栄養素も補え、食感もいい。
Multigrain Rice: This rice contains dozens of grains such as black rice, barley, common millet, and Japanese millet and is widely popular in health-conscious Japan.

餅米
Mochigome
お餅はもちろん、赤飯、ちまき、炊き込みごはんなどに使う。甘みが特徴。
Glutinous Rice: Characteristically sweet, this rice is used to make mochi rice cake as well as chimaki (rice dumpling wrapped in bamboo leaves), and takikomi Gohan (mixed rice).

基本の朝ごはん　　The Basics of Breakfast

002 味噌汁
Miso-shiru

昔から味噌は医者いらずといわれるように、日本人の健康に貢献してきた発酵食品のひとつ。せめて一日一回はお味噌汁を飲んでほしいと思います。鰹節や煮干しでだしをとらなくても、食材から出るだしを活かすこともできます。冷蔵庫にある残りものや納豆などなんでも入れてOK。特にトマトは味噌との相性も抜群で、バターを少し落とすとパンにも合う味噌汁に。私は寒い季節には白味噌、夏の暑い時期には赤だしが飲みたくなります。自由自在な組合せで、思いつきや体が感じるままに作ってみると、味噌汁の世界が変わってくること間違いなしです。

Miso Soup: Fewer people drink miso soup nowadays but miso has such a high nutritional value even among fermented products of soybean that the saying, "Miso keeps the doctor away," exists. A variety of miso is produced in areas with differing climates and environments. As the seasons transition, you may change the ingredients or switch up the type of miso paste. Follow your instinct and experiment with different ingredients and miso to explore the world of miso soup. **Recipe➡ P.154**

赤だしの味噌汁
Akadashi no Miso-shiru
八丁味噌に米味噌を合わせた赤味噌仕立ての味噌汁。コクのあるだしをしっかりとるのがコツ。写真の具は油揚げと豆腐。あさりやシジミも合う。
Red Miso Soup: When using this miso, the key lies in extracting rich dashi stock to balance off the strong miso flavor. The ingredients here consist of deep-fried tofu pouches and tofu. Clams and shijimi (freshwater clams) go well with this miso too.

白味噌の味噌汁
Shiro Miso no Miso-shiru
白味噌は甘さととろみが特長で、冬場に体が温まる味噌汁。写真の具は蕪とワカメ。里芋もおすすめ。からしを隠し味に入れると美味しい。
White Miso Soup: It is characterized by its sweetness and thickness, which makes for hearty miso soup that warms you up in the winter. It also goes well with turnip and wakame; as a secret ingredient to spice up the flavor, add a hint of karashi mustard.

米味噌の味噌汁
Kome Miso no Miso-shiru
一般的によく使われている田舎味噌で、煮干しのだしでも合う。豚汁などにもおすすめ。写真の具はナスとネギ。
Brown Miso Soup: This uses the common inaka miso, literally meaning "countryside miso," which goes well with dashi stock taken from niboshi (dried sardines). It's also recommended for ton-jiru (pork and vegetable miso soup). The ingredients here are eggplant and green onion.

Red Miso Soup

White Miso Soup

Brown Miso Soup

003 焼き魚
Yaki Zakana

焼くだけで簡単にメインになる手軽な魚料理。鯵や秋刀魚、鯖などに含まれる豊富なDHAがとれるのもいいですね。干物はナンプラーをかけて焼くと臭みが半減します。身をほぐしてごはんに混ぜても美味しいです。

Grilled Fish: Some shy away from dried fish or grilled fish because of the required grill cleaning or amount of smoke, but it's actually an easy main dish. Fish like horse mackerel, saury, and chub mackerel make a great accessible source of DHA too.

004 おひたし
Ohitashi

さっと湯がいたほうれん草や小松菜におかかをのせる、あっという間にできるおひたし料理。ゆでて小分けにし、冷凍しておくと、使いたい分だけすぐに使えて便利です。

Boiled Vegetable: Boiled leafy greens can be quickly made by boiling spinach or mustard spinach then sprinkling some bonito flakes for topping. Top with dashi or soy sauce to bring out the quality of the ingredients to your liking.

005 漬物
Tsukemono

伝統的な野菜の漬物の多くは、粕漬け、麹漬け、もろみ漬け、味噌漬け、醤油漬けなど、発酵食品に漬けこんで作ります。残り野菜と味噌をポリ袋に入れてよく揉み、一晩寝かすだけで、手軽に自家製漬物の出来上がり。翌日の食卓にすぐ出せます。

Pickles: Whether it's nuka-zuke (rice bran pickles), miso-zuke (miso pickles), rakkyo-zuke (pickled shallots) or umeboshi (pickled sour plum), pickles and fermented foods offer a world of options. That each region has pickles cultivated in their respective climates speaks to Japan's unique fermentation culture. They make for a perfect last bite at the end of a meal.

006 納豆
Natto

ネバネバの納豆菌の健康効果が評価され、近年、納豆の消費が増えているそうです。オクラやモロヘイヤを足してネバネバをアップさせ、そうめんにかけるのもおすすめ。漬物を刻んで混ぜたバクダン納豆も冷やっこと相性抜群です。

Fermented Soy Beans: A traditional food eaten since ancient times, natto has been recognized for the health benefits of its bacillus natto, and now serves one of the health food staples in Japan. It's also known as a litmus test to see if a foreigner is truly a Japanese foodie depending on whether they can eat the smelly natto or not.

| 基本の朝ごはん | The Basics of Breakfast |

007　だし巻き卵
Dashi-maki Tamago

だし巻き卵は朝ごはんに限らず、お弁当にも名脇役として欠かせない存在。私流は、砂糖、醤油、酒、みりんに、たっぷりのだしを入れてふわふわと形を作っていくやり方。卵液を3回に分け、スクランブルエッグを作るように箸でかき混ぜながらよせ、空気を入れるように折りたたんで焼いていきます。中がしっとりと柔らかく、口の中でじゅわっと甘みとだしが混じりあう、やさしい口当たりのだし巻き卵ができあがります。

Japanese Rolled Omelet: Dashi-maki tamago has the power to put a smile on everyone's face. A popular side dish that you can never get sick of, it's not limited to breakfast and serves as an essential supporting role in bento (lunch box) meals. My recipe uses plenty of dashi to create a fluffy shape. With one bite the sweetness and dashi blend perfectly together, getting you hooked on it for more. Whether it's adding extra soy sauce or a dash of sugar, each family's mother has her own special dashi-maki tamago recipe. **Recipe➡P.154**

定番ごはん
Staple Dishes

定番のごはんは、ひとくちにいうと「何でもない日のごはん」。
時と場所を問わず、ランチや夕飯、居酒屋のメニューにもよく登場する
みんなが大好きで気楽に食べられるもの。
好きだからよく作る、好きだからよく食べる、
登場回数が多い安定した人気のごはん
といったところでしょうか。

Staple dishes may be summed up as meals for ordinary days. No matter the time or place, these dishes are loved by all and are frequently served at lunch, dinner, or at izakayas (Japanese pubs). As all-time favorites, they are made and eaten often, maintaining their popularity as heavy rotations.

23

定番ごはん | Staple Dishes

008 卵かけごはん
Tamago-kake Gohan

新鮮な卵が手に入ったら即卵かけごはん！が昔からの私の決まり。お醤油はちょっと甘みのあるもの、柚子胡椒を少しのせ、ピリ辛感を味わいます。

Egg Raw over Rice: If you can get a hold of fresh eggs, the immediate answer is egg raw over rice! This dish's lifeline is the egg. Nowadays, you can buy soy sauce suited for egg raw over rice. It's the classic simple meal.

009 茶漬け
Chazuke

私のお茶漬けに欠かせないのは、香ばしくて美味しい京都のぶぶあられ。焼いた鮭と、海苔とぶぶあられをかけて、だしで頂く、ベストマッチな組合せです。

Soup over Rice: Made by pouring dashi stock or tea over rice, it offers a world of options, with a variety of toppings from pickles, sour plum, salmon, to high quality sea bream.

010 炊き込みごはん
Takikomi Gohan

春は筍やグリーンピース、夏は枝豆、秋は栗、冬は里芋などと、季節の野菜で素朴に作る炊き込みごはん。旬の素材そのものの良さを楽しめます。

Mixed Rice: This dish provides infinite possibilities just by simply cooking ingredients and rice together. Savor it by combining seasonal ingredients. **Recipe ➡ P.154**

011 赤飯
Sekihan

餅米に小豆やささげを入れて炊いたごはん。赤いものは邪気を払うといわれ、昔からご祝儀などハレの日の食卓に登場してきました。蒸すのが一般的ですが、炊飯器や土鍋でも、もっちりでほくほくのお赤飯が簡単にできます。

Red Bean Rice: Glutinous rice cooked with azuki beans and cowpea, is traditionally served on festive days since red items are said to rid one of bad spirits. Although it is generally steamed, you can also easily prepare it with a rice cooker or a microwave.

Thick Wheat Noodles

そうめん
Somen

室町時代にはすでに食されていたというそうめん。ゆでた後に氷水でしっかりもみ洗いすると、シコシコの麺に仕上がります。夏の定番ですが、暑い時こそ煮麺にするのもオツなもの。卵と梅干しを入れて、はふはふと食べるのが最高です。

Since the noodles boil quickly, it's an efficient go-to dish in the summer that can be served in no time. To achieve the perfect al dente texture, wash the noodles with cold running water after boiling.

蕎麦
Soba

一方、蕎麦の歴史は奈良時代からとも。蕎麦は小麦の麺に比べ栄養価が高く、中に含まれるルチンは健康・美容効果もあり、スーパーフードとして再評価されています。噛み切らずにすすって食べることで、のどに抜ける蕎麦の香りを楽しみます。

Buckwheat Noodles: Nutritious noodles that are said to have originated in the Nara period. Slurp without chewing too much to enjoy the aroma of soba sliding down your throat. Ask for the "sobayu," the hot water that the soba was cooked in, to add to the remaining stock to drink.

うどん
Udon

うどんが今のように長い麺になったのは江戸時代に入ってから。地域によって汁の味、麺の形状は様々。私は麺にコシがある讃岐うどん派。天カスと海苔をゆで玉にのせ、お醤油味で食べるのが気に入っています。

Thick Wheat Noodles: Udon reached its current form of long noodles in the Edo period. The flavor of the stock and the noodle shape vary by region. The popular Sanuki udon's secret lies in its chewy elasticity; it's all about the firm and slippery texture.

| 定番ごはん | Staple Dishes

冷やし中華
Hiyashi Chuka

食欲が減退する暑い夏に、何回食べても飽きない麺がこれ。ゆで麺にまずたれをからめると、麺にしっかり味がしみ込みます。モヤシときゅうりのシンプルなトッピングのシャリシャリ感が意外とよく合いますよ。

Cold Ramen: During the hot summer when your appetite decreases, this noodle dish will help you out. Soy sauce, sesame sauce, and vinegar help boost your appetite. Add plenty of vegetables and proteins like eggs, chicken, or pork for a well-balanced meal.

ラーメン
Ramen

中国が起源のラーメンも、いまや日本を代表する国民的な麺に。つゆを少なめにし、ポン酢、ラー油を加えて、サンラータン風味にしたラーメンも酸っぱ辛い味が食欲をそそります。炒めた野菜をたっぷり入れると美味しさ倍増です。

Everyone gets a sudden craving for ramen. Originating in China, Japanese ramen has developed from a national noodle dish to a worldwide favorite. With stock like soy sauce, miso, and pork bone available, which ramen style do you choose?

焼きそば
Yakisoba

私の好きな焼きそばは、肉は入れずに、細かく切ったさつま揚げとたっぷりなキャベツを入れる変わり焼きそば。ボリューム満点なので、麺は少なめにします。

Stir Fried Noodles: Yakisoba can't escape its snack-like supporting role since it's often eaten in food stalls. Mix steamed noodles, vegetables, and meat with plenty of Worcester sauce to serve this classic; don't forget the essential dried green laver and pickled ginger.

Cold Ramen

Ramen

Stir Fried Noodles

定番ごはん | Staple Dishes

018 天丼
Tendon

天ぷらだけでも美味しいですが、甘ダレがかかるだけで別の美味しさが広がる天丼。食べやすさを優先して、うちではもっぱら海老、イカを入れたかき揚げ丼です。夏野菜のパプリカやズッキーニも彩りがよいのでよく使います。

Tempura Bowl: Simple tempura alone is delicious enough, but pouring some sweet sauce over it adds a whole new layer of flavors. Either crispy or sauce-soaked batter go well with the rice. Any ingredient, from shrimp, eggplant, lotus root, to kaki-age (mixed vegetables) can turn into tempura.

019 カツ丼
Katsudon

サクサクのカツの上にとろとろの卵、このハーモニーが美味しい丼。カツは8割がた揚がったところで引き上げて、揚げすぎないのがコツです。肉を薄切りにし、下に千切りキャベツをしき、ソースをかけるソースカツ丼も美味しいのでお試しを。

Pork Cutlet Bowl: The perfectly satisfying rice bowl's secret lies in the delicious harmony of a soft egg over a freshly fried cutlet. In Japan, eating lots of "katsu" (which also means "to win") on a big day is said to bring good luck.

020 牛丼
Gyudon

牛肉とネギを煮込んだ牛鍋が牛丼の原点だといわれています。ちょっと高めの美味しい牛肉と玉ねぎに千切り生姜を加え、だし汁や旨み調味料は入れず、水、砂糖、酒、みりん、醤油だけで味付けした自家製牛丼は格別です。

Beef Bowl: The prime example of rice bowl dishes, gyudon has firmly established itself as an easy dining option. When cooking at home, pour plenty of sauce to allow the rice to soak it up. Vigorously savoring it makes it all the more delicious. **Recipe➡P.155**

021 親子丼
Oyakodon

明治の頃、鶏鍋の〆として卵をおとして食べたのが始まりとか。家庭で作る時のポイントは、卵液を2回に分けて入れること。ふわふわの仕上がりになります。火の入れすぎにはくれぐれも要注意。

Chicken and Egg Bowl: Oyakodon (literally "parent and child" rice bowl) made by simmering chicken and onions with warishita (stock mixed with soy sauce, mirin, and sugar) and pouring beaten eggs. Separate the eggs in two batches to yield a fluffy texture.

定番ごはん | Staple Dishes

Japanese Savory Pancake

Octopus Balls

022 お好み焼き
Okonomiyaki

小麦粉に好みの具材を入れて焼くので、「お好み焼き」と名がついたそうです。原点は、千利休が茶会の菓子として出した「麩の焼」ともいわれていますが、いまのかたちになったのは戦後のようです。私は大阪風が好みです。

Japanese Savory Pancake: The name "okonomiyaki" comes from grilling (yaki) "what you like" (okonomi) with flour. The ingredients and grilling style vary by region. Though the Kansai and Hiroshima style are some of the most well known, each family can craft their original okonomiyaki.

023 たこ焼き
Takoyaki

大阪では一家に一台あるというたこ焼き器。なぜか我が家にも昔、ガス式のたこ焼き器がありました。種はゆるめに作り、たことネギ、紅生姜を入れます。金串の代わりにキリを使ってひっくり返していたことが、子ども時代の楽しい思い出です。

Octopus Balls: Originating from Osaka, takoyaki is a bite-size flour dish with chopped octopus inside. Enjoy a freshly prepared batch with plenty of sauce, red ginger, and laver. As Osaka's soul food, it's common to keep a takoyaki pan at home.

定番ごはん | Staple Dishes

024 お弁当
Obento

お弁当作りは「五色五味」を基本に考えるのが大事。彩りよいお弁当は栄養バランスもよく食欲もそそられます。でも、毎日のお弁当作りは大変。私はハンバーグを小さく作って残したり、タネをピーマンの肉詰めにアレンジしたりと、晩のおかずを二段活用。ひじきや切り干し大根、マカロニサラダやポテトサラダなどの作り置きも力強い味方になります。

Lunch Box: As a portable single meal, you can pack a balanced and nutritious meal to your liking. Bento's popularity is growing overseas as well. Whether it's bento for cherry blossom hanami season, day-to-day school lunches, or ekiben style sold exclusively at local train stations in Japan, the possibilities are endless.

025 おにぎり
Onigiri

季節の具材や冷蔵庫の残り物でも作れるおにぎりのバリエーションは多種多様。枝豆と塩昆布は私の定番の組合せ。最近ハマっているのが、海苔の代わりにおぼろ昆布で包むおにぎり。おぼろ昆布がごはんの水分をほどよく吸ってくれ、ほわっと美味しくなります。ルッコラを刻んで塩だけでにぎるのも、意外な美味しさ！

Rice Ball: Onigiri offers a range of shapes and flavors, whether it's mixing rice with ingredients, filling the inside, or creating triangular, barrel, or round shapes. As it lasts long time, it's an essential Japanese food for bentos and gatherings, and is becoming an international hit.

人気の一品
Popular Meals

和食の人気メニューには、
外国から入り日本風にアレンジされ
家庭の味として定着したものが
たくさんあります。
その和洋折衷の味は
みんなが大好きな洋食、
昔ながらのおふくろの味、
居酒屋メニューなどとして
バリエーション豊かに
受け継がれています。

Many popular Japanese dishes are imported recipes arranged Japanese-style that have become staples of home cooking. Ranging across Western-style food that pleases the crowd, side dishes reminiscent of the taste of mom's cooking, and menus inspired by izakaya dining, this Japanese-Western hybrid taste is ever-evolving into an international favorite.

人気の一品 | Popular Meals

026 ハンバーグ
Hambagu

私がふだん作るのはミニバーグ。火の通りが早いので時短にもなります。肉の分量を少し減らして、高野豆腐をすりおろして入れると、ヘルシーで低カロリーな仕上がりに。

Japanese Salisbury Steak: From children to adults, everyone loves hambagu. Pour rich demi-glace sauce for western style, or top it with grated Japanese radish and soy sauce for Japanese style; you can enjoy it in a million ways depending on the finishing sauce.

027 生姜焼き
Shogayaki

玉ねぎと生姜をすりおろし、醤油、酒、みりんに肉をつけ込んで焼くと、玉ねぎの甘みが出て美味しくなります。隠し味に少しお酢を入れるとまろやかさも加わります。

Ginger Pork: Shogayaki is one of the most popular dishes especially for business lunch breaks. Ginger and pork make a perfect match and boost your appetite. It's delicious cooked. Either thick or thin slices of meat. **Recipe➡P.155**

028 ナポリタン
Naporitan

日本化したスパゲティの代表格といえばナポリタン。ウスターソースを隠し味に使うと、ケチャップの甘みがおさえられます。目玉焼きをのせると懐かしさがぐっと倍増しますよ。

Spaghetti Napolitana: Spaghetti Napolitana comes first to mind when considering Japanese style spaghetti. Stir fry onion, green pepper, and wiener sausage, then garnish with ketchup for the signature flavor. It's a classic at kissaten (Japanese-style cafes.)
Recipe➡P.155

 ### カレーライス
Kare-raisu

明治初期に英国海軍を通じて入った海軍カレーが起源といわれている、国民食のカレー。夏はナス、ズッキーニの素揚げ、フライドオニオンなどをトッピングするなど、カレーで季節を楽しむのもまた一興です。

Curry Rice: Curry rice can be considered Japan's national food. The dish originates from navy curry that was imported through the British Navy in the early Meiji period. Each family creates its own recipe for the sauce using various ingredients. Creat your own family's special curry!

| Popular Meals

餃子
Gyoza

失敗しない餃子の焼き方は、冷たいフライパンに餃子を並べ、中火で少し焦げ目をつけた後に、ひたひたにお湯を入れてフタをし、強火で一気に蒸し焼きに。最後に油を少しまわし入れ弱火で焼くと、パリパリ餃子の出来上がりです。

Pan Fried Dumplings: Japanese gyoza refers to fried dumplings, but in the authentic Chinese style, steamed dumplings reign supreme. Gyoza packs in the delicious textural harmony of crispiness, stickiness, and juiciness and pairs perfectly well with rice and beer.

肉じゃが
Nikujaga

カレーと同様に日本の海軍由来の料理だった肉じゃが。新じゃがの季節には、素揚げしてから肉と煮込みます。コクが出てさらに美味しい仕上がりに。

Meat and Potato Stew: A signature home-cooked Japanese dish, nikujaga combines delicious meat and sweet onions, allowing them to soak into the soft potatoes. Same as curry rice, the dish was brought in by the Japanese Navy.

032 コロッケ
Korokke

揚げた時にコロッケが割れてしまってがっかりということがあります。それを解決するには、じゃがいもの粗熱をしっかり冷ましてから形を作ること。じゃがいもをたっぷりめに入れると、ホクホク感もアップします。

Croquette: Croquette is boiled and mashed potatoes combined with ingredients such as ground meat and then fried. Originating from French croquettes, it's now a popular western style home-cooked dish. It's best served when freshly fried.

033 から揚げ
Kara-age

毎日のお弁当、行楽、パーティにも出番の多いおかず。つけダレをちょっと変えて、エスニック風にホットサワーソース、味噌マヨで和風味にと、から揚げの七変化を楽しんでいます。

Japanese Fried Chicken: Crispy on the outside and juicy on the inside, kara-age bursts with fragrant soy sauce flavor. As everyone's favorite, it's one of the most frequently served side dishes, perfect for bento lunch boxes, events, and parties.

人気の一品 | Popular Meals

034 金目の煮付け
Kinme no Nitsuke

色も鮮やかで見ためも美しいので縁起物としても人気が高い金目鯛。煮付けにしても歯ごたえある食感が楽しめます。煮る前に熱湯をかけ、臭み抜きをするのがポイントです。

Braised Alfonsino: Alfonsino is rich in fat but also offers a firm texture. If fresh, sashimi would be best, but due to the strong smell it's most suited for simmering. With its vibrant colors and appearance, it's popularly known to bring good luck.

035 鯖味噌
Saba Miso

鯖はクセの強い魚。酒と味噌で煮ることで、鯖の臭みを消す効果があるといわれてます。煮込む際は、落とし蓋をして味をしみこませます。一度冷ましてから、二度煮込むとしっかり鯖に味がつきます。

Mackerel Braised in Miso: Braise the mackerel fillet with ingredients such as miso, sugar, sake, mirin, and ginger. The miso effectively removes the mackerel smell. It boasts an unbeatable popularity at Japanese style diners (teishokuya). **Recipe➡P.156**

036 ぶりの照り焼き
Buri no Teriyaki

照り焼きの甘ダレは何にでも応用できますが、ぶりのような魚は長く漬けすぎると、逆に臭みがでるので気をつけましょう。30分漬けおわったら、片面10分ずつフライパンで焼き、煮汁は煮込んでとろみをつけて、上からかけます。

Yellowtail Teriyaki: Teriyaki refers to grilling fish or meat while layering a sweet sauce using soy sauce. As yellowtail holds different names for each stage of growth, it's popularly eaten to bring good career luck.

037 刺身
Sashimi

新鮮な旬の魚は、シンプルに刺身で味わうのが一番。でも、帆立などひと手間を加えることによって、さらに美味しく頂けるものもあります。表面を炙るか、熱湯で霜降りにしてから切ると、甘みがぐっと増すのです。

Whether red fish, white fish, blue fish, or shellfish, fresh seasonal fish is best served simple sashimi style. However, as the slicing technique determines the taste, mastering the skill is essential.

45

人気の一品 | Popular Meals

038 きんぴらごぼう
Kinpira Gobo

ごぼうの歯ごたえをしっかり残したい時はマッチ棒大に切ります。また、ごぼうに皮を残すことで、さらに食感がアップします。酒、砂糖、醤油の調味料で甘辛く炒めるだけのシンプルな調理法は、レンコン、セロリなどにも使え、常備菜としても重宝します。

Braised Burdock Root and Carrot: Kinpira is known as a pre-prepared dish that goes well with rice. The tip is to not overcook, preserving the burdock's texture. It's a simple recipe just using sake, sugar, and soy sauce to braise with a sweet and spicy taste. Depending on how you cut the burdock roots and carrots, the dish can have a bold or delicate finish.

039 胡麻和え
Goma-ae

ほうれん草はもちろん、青菜やインゲンなど旬の野菜で手軽に作れる一品。胡麻の香りが野菜の美味しさをアップするので、私は練り胡麻と半すり胡麻を合わせ、砂糖、醤油、みりんで味付けします。かまぼこやチクワなどと合わせるとバリエーションも広がります。

Spinach with Sesame Sauce: Easy to prepare with seasonal greens and beans, the sesame aroma boosts the taste of the vegetables. In addition to sugar, soy sauce and miso may be added to taste.

040 ポテトサラダ
Poteto Sarada

我が家の、お店の、それぞれオリジナルがあるのがポテトサラダ。じゃがいもが熱いうちに、酢、砂糖、塩、胡椒、そして、私は隠し味に粒マスタードを入れます。全体が冷めてから、最後にマヨネーズを入れるのがポイントです。

Potato Salad: Whether it's in your family's kitchen or your favorite restaurant, each kitchen carries its own original potato salad recipe. For bento lunch or breakfast, this dish comes in handy at any meal of the day. Although nothing special, it brings a smile to the table. The secret ingredient in my home recipe is mustard.

041 鶏の照焼
Tori no Teriyaki

同量の砂糖、みりん、醤油で作る照り焼きソース。この基本を押さえておくと鶏肉だけでなく、他の食材にも使える、簡単で便利な万能ソースです。煮詰めるとツヤが出て照り感が増します。鶏とオレンジの相性がいいので、私はソースにマーマレードをいれています。

Chicken Teriyaki: Teriyaki sauce—made with the same amount of sugar, mirin, and soy sauce—is a versatile sauce that can be used for other ingredients besides chicken. Boiled down, the sauce increases its glossy look. This simple and quick cooking method creates a highly satisfying and rich meal. **Recipe➡P.156**

042 焼き鳥
Yakitori

串に刺さった焼き鳥の形ができたのは、屋台文化全盛の明治の頃のようです。居酒屋の定番の一品ですが、我が家では昔からお土産の定番でした。残りものは、おにぎりの具材や、サラダのトッピングなどにリメイクしてます。

Chicken Skewers: Yakitori serves the everyday people; wherever you go, an izakaya offers it on their menu. A casual finger food, it must be threaded on skewers. Enjoy it salt-grilled, with sweet and spicy sauce, or by switching it up for different chicken parts.

043 枝豆
Edamame

意外と難しいのがゆで方。まず、すり鉢に枝豆と多めの塩を入れ軽くしごき、うぶ毛をとります。沸騰したお湯に枝豆を入れ、再び沸騰させて5〜7分。硬さをみて、ざるにあげて広げます。うちわを使い一気に冷ますと緑色がきれいに仕上がります。

Edamame is immature soybeans harvested when young. By boiling with salt or steaming, it serves as a tasty snack or ingredient. Nowadays edamame is gaining fans all over the world for its healthiness.

044 山かけ
Yamakake

山芋をすりおろして、刺身や和えものにかけたものを山かけといいます。独特なネバネバ感のある山芋は栄養価が高く、疲労回復に効果大。すりおろす時に手がかゆくなるのを防ぐには、手に薄めた酢水をつけると効果的です。

Tuna with Grated Yam: Yamakake is grated yam poured on sashimi or dressed dishes (aemono). With a unique slimy texture, yam contains high nutritional value and promotes recovery from fatigue.

045 冷奴
Hiyayakko

豆腐に薬味をのせ、醤油をかけて頂くというシンプルを極めた一品。豆腐の種類もたくさんありますが、私は大豆の香りが残ったものが好きで、オリーブオイルと塩をかけるのが、最近のお気に入りの食べ方です。

Chilled Tofu: Tofu's history goes back to the Edo period. For this simple dish, enjoy the variety of condiments and sauces available as garnish.

| 人気の一品 | Popular Meals

046　惣菜パン
Sozai Pan

カレーパンとコロッケパンが、はじめて世の中に登場したのは昭和の始めだそうです。私は忙しい時は、残りもののおかず、コロッケ、サラダなどをささっとパンにはさんで、即席の総菜パンをお昼にしています。写真の左から、コーンをマヨネーズで和えてチーズをのせたマヨコーンパン、カレーパン、卵サラダパンとツナサラダパン。揚げものを使った白身魚フライパンとコロッケパン。不動の人気やきそばパン、ごぼうサラダパン、ほうれん草グラタンパン。

Bread Meals: Sozai pan involves sandwiching side dish (sozai) ingredients in the buns (pan) or layering them on top. Staples such as curry bread and croquette bread were first introduced in the beginning of the Showa period. From left to right: mayonnaise-corn bread topped with cheese, curry bread, egg salad bread, and tuna salad bread; fish fry bread and croquette bread for fried fillings; yakisoba bread, burdock root salad bread, and spinach gratin bread.

| 人気の一品 | Popular Meals

047 中華まん
Chukaman

その名のとおり中国の饅頭が起源で、大正時代に、肉詰め饅頭を略して「肉まん」として広まったといいます。コンビニの冬の風物詩となって久しいですが、毎シーズン新しい味の百花繚乱。私は中高生に人気のピザまんを目当てに。

Chinese Steamed Buns: Chukaman is steamed buns with filling wrapped in soft dough. Nikuman (steamed pork bun) and anman (steamed red bean paste bun) being most common, steamed buns have established themselves as store-bought bites rather than homemade food. Recently, kareman (steamed curry bun) and pizaman (steamed pizza bun) have become popular at convenience stores.

肉まん Nikuman

中華まんの王道。豚挽肉、筍、玉ねぎ、椎茸などの具を中華風に味付け。

Steamed Pork Bun: The king of Chinese steamed buns contain fillings such as minced pork, bamboo, and onions that are thickened and seasoned Chinese-style.

あんまん Anman

小豆を炊き上げ、黒胡麻風味をつけたこしあんと、ふわっとした皮が相性抜群。

Steamed Red Bean Paste Bun: The red bean paste made from cooked adzuki is slightly seasoned with black sesame, which perfectly matches the fluffy skin of the bun.

ピザまん Pizaman

ピザソースの旨みがほどよく皮にしみこんで、まさに和洋折衷の代表例。

Steamed Pizza Bun: A popular and one-of-a-kind Chinese steamed bun, it contains pizza ingredients as fillings such as bacon and tomato sauce.

カレーまん kareman

変わり種中華まんのトップバッターとして30年以上前に登場。誰もが大好きなカレー味。

Steamed Curry Bun: As one of the frontrunners of unusual Chinese steamed buns, it was introduced over 30 years ago. The filling is everyone's favorite meat curry.

ごちそうごはん
Festive Meals

人が集まってみんなでワイワイ一緒に食べると美味しさも増し、盛り上がるごちそうごはん。
具材を揃えるだけで、あとは巻くだけの手巻き寿司や
目の前で調理しながらプロセスそのものも楽しめる鍋料理などは、
一つのものをみんなで頂く楽しさが、最大の調味料です。
我が家の気軽にできるおもてなしごはんを紹介します。

When everyone eats a festive meal together for special gatherings and occasions, it tastes even better and warms up the scene.
Whether it's hand-rolled sushi that only requires you to lay out the ingredients, or hot pot that lets you enjoy the cooking process at the dinner table, many recipes involve little effort to host and entertain guests.

048 手巻き寿司
Temaki-zushi

パーティなどで手軽にできるごちそうごはんの一つ。刺身のほかに、お年寄りから子どもまで一緒に楽しめる具材のアレンジとして、フライやローストビーフ、納豆、漬物などを用意してみては？巻く時は寿司飯の量を少なめに調整するのがポイントです。

Hand-Rolled Sushi: Temaki sushi makes for an easy festive meal for large gatherings and parties. Prepare sumeshi (vinegared sushi rice), sashimi, vegetables of your choice, seasoning, and seaweed, then choose the ingredients to hand-roll and eat. Whether it's fried food, meat, or cooked dishes, anything can be used for filling to create a different kind of temaki sushi. From children to adults, everyone can enjoy this popular sushi dish together.

❶ 海苔（サイズは1/4、1/2どちらでも）を手のひらにのせ、真ん中にごはんを薄く広げる。
Place a piece of nori (either halved or quartered) in your hand and thinly spread the rice in the middle.

❷ 薬味のシソなどをのせた上に、刺身類、ツマ類を一緒にのせる。具材の取り合わせはお好みで。
After placing condiments such as shiso, top it with sashimi and garnishes. Mix and match the ingredients to your liking.

❸ 具材を海苔の両側から包み込んで巻く。具材を欲張りすぎると巻けないので注意。
Wrap the nori from both ends to roll up the ingredients. Be careful not to overload; leave enough space for the nori to wrap around the ingredients.

❹ 巻き上げたら、逆さにして上の部分にお醤油をつけて頂く。
Once it's rolled up, turn it upside down and dip the top part in soy sauce.

049　天ぷら
Tempura

天ぷらは蕎麦・寿司と並んで、江戸三昧といわれた名物料理です。サクッと揚がらないと天ぷらに苦手意識を持つ人も多いようですが、ポイントは油の量を多くすること。そして衣は粘らないようにざっくりと混ぜること、衣と食材は冷たくしておくこと。また、衣は少なめに作り、最後はかき揚げにして使い切ります。卓上電気フライヤーを使い、目の前で揚げるのも楽しいですね。

Although tempura is served at long-established specialty restaurants, you can also easily make it at home. Dip seafood or vegetables in batter made from flour mixed with eggs and water, then fry them. Serve with tentsuyu (about three parts dashi, one part mirin, and one part soy sauce) and grated daikon. Along with soba and sushi, tempura is known as one of the "Edo no Zanmai," or local dishes of Edo; it's globally as popular as sushi. Vegetable-only tempura is called shojin-age. Electric countertop fryers come in handy too.

ごちそうごはん | Festive Meals

すき焼き
Sukiyaki

美味しいお肉を家で食べる時は、やっぱりすき焼きが一番。特に、我が家では大晦日に一年の感謝をすき焼きで締めくくります。辛めの割り下が好きだった父と、甘め好きな母で家族談義が盛りあがり、ワイワイと賑やかな食卓になるのが常。最近は、溜まり醤油だけで頂くすき焼きが、肉そのものの味を楽しむことができて、気に入っています。すき焼きはそれぞれの家庭の思い出の味ですね。

Simmer beef with onions, tofu, or shirataki (yam-starch noodles) in salty-sweet seasoning such as soy sauce and sugar then dip it in raw egg to serve sukiyaki, a hot pot dish that suits a special family meal. Although it's known for having different recipes by region, juicy and salty-sweet beef is essential. Sukiyaki has developed into a world-famous dish; Kyu Sakamoto's "Ue o Muite Arukou" (literally "I Look Up as I Walk") is known as "Sukiyaki Song". Recipe☞P.156

051 寄せ鍋
Yosenabe

寒い冬には部屋も温まる鍋が最高のごちそうで、豚肉とほうれん草のしゃぶしゃぶ風常夜鍋、キムチ鍋、かに鍋などが我が家の食卓によく登場します。いろいろな具材を寄せて入れることが寄せ鍋の由来。最近は豆乳やトマトをベースした変わり鍋も登場しています。どんな鍋でも最後の楽しみは締めの雑炊。大麦を入れるヘルシーな麦雑炊がマイブームです。

Mixed Hot Pot: During the cold winter, a warm yosenabe makes the best feast. Even if it's called yosenabe, ingredients including local specialties vary by region. The name yosenabe comes from mixing an assortment of things together. The basics involve stewing seafood such as cod, salmon, and shrimp, vegetables such as Chinese cabbage, green onion, and edible chrysanthemum, mushrooms and tofu in dashi stock, then serving with condiments and sauce. After enjoying a plethora of ingredients, another joy awaits in adding rice or udon to the hot pot at the end of the meal. The chef in charge of the hot pot process is referred to as nabe-bugyo, literally meaning hot pot commissioner.

しゃぶしゃぶ
Shabu-shabu

しゃぶしゃぶは「牛肉の水炊き」が原型で、戦後に広まったそうです。だしの中で牛肉を洗うように火を通すのでその擬音が名の由来とか。高級鍋料理というイメージですが、家庭でも簡単にできるのがしゃぶしゃぶの良さ。ピーラーでおろした薄切り大根と肉をいっしょに、白ごまダレにラー油とネギを入れたピリ辛ダレにつけて食べるのも、相性抜群でおすすめです。

Shabu-shabu is a hot pot dish served at the dinner table that involves quickly immersing very thinly-sliced beef in boiling stock, then dipping it in sauce. Ponzu (citrus-based sauce) and sesame sauce are most commonly used for the sauce. Pork or seafood can be used instead of beef. Shabu-shabu is served at restaurants but also in households when people gather for an occasion. After the meat, add the vegetables, Chinese cabbage, mizuna (Japanese mustard greens), carrots, and mushrooms. Ice shabu-shabu meat after dipping in boiling stock to make cold shabu-shabu, a popular dish for the summer.

ごちそうごはん | Festive Meals

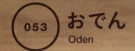

おでん
Oden

もともとは江戸の豆腐田楽、大阪のこんにゃく田楽が起源といわれているおでん。冬になると味のしみ込んだ大根が無性に食べたくなります。大根にだしの味をしっかりつけるには、下ゆでと十字隠し包丁を入れること。ひと手間が美味しさを導きます。また、他の具材も味のしみにくいものから時間差をつけて、弱火で煮崩れしないように煮込むのがコツです。

Oden originated from tofu dengaku (grilled tofu) from Edo and konnyaku dengaku (grilled konnyaku) from Osaka. Initially served in stalls or candy shops, it gained popularity as a homecooked meal as fish-paste products became more accessible. In kelp and bonito stock, stew daikon, eggs, konnyaku, hampen (fish cakes), and chikuwa (fish sausage), then serve with Japanese mustard. The trick is to slowly cook the ingredients in the stock's low heat.

季節のごはん
Seasonal Dishes

子どもの頃、お正月やひな祭りといった年中行事はワクワクするものでした。
大人になり、伝統的な行事には、一年をとおして季節に寄り添い、
自然を尊び、家族の健康と幸せを願う気持ちが込められていることを知りました。
昔からの風習を守り伝えていく大切な日本の歳時記と行事ごはん。
もう一度、一緒におさらいしてみませんか。

Japan's traditional events are focused on staying attuned to the four seasons and respecting nature with care. Festive meals, which are important in protecting and passing on old customs, always embody a wish for one's family's health and happiness.

季節のごはん | Seasonal Dishes

【 1月1日 】
お正月
Oshogatsu

正月の「正す」という言葉には
「あらためなおす」「初め」の意味があります。
お正月は新しい一年の幸せや豊作をもたらす
年神様をお迎えする大きな行事として、
昔から大切に祝われてきました。
年末の大掃除、正月飾りをはじめ、鏡餅、
お正月料理の準備を終え、元旦を迎えます。
我が家は鯛の姿焼き、小豆ごはんを並べ、
家族全員でお節料理を囲み、
お屠蘇の前に福茶を頂くことが習わしです。

New Year's Day, January 1

New Year's Day, January 1st, is the most
important day of the year. In the Japanese kanji
character for Oshogatsu, the Sho part represents
the word "to correct," which can also mean "to
mend," or "the beginning." Oshogatsu has long
been cherished as the first month to restart with
a new year. For New Year's Day, the entire family
gathers around osechi ryori (traditional Japanese
New Year foods), drinks otoso (spiced medicinal
sake) and eats zoni (rice cake and vegetable
soup).

季節のごはん | Seasonal Dishes

054 お節
Osechi

お節料理とは、その年の豊作や家内安全、子孫繁栄を願う意味を込めて作る祝い膳です。重箱に詰めるのは"めでたさを重ねる"という意味があり、料理の品数も縁起のいい奇数が基本。一般的なのは四段重ねで、上から順に、一の重、二の重、三の重、与の重、地方や家庭ごとにお重の詰め方は様々のようです。近年は三段重ねが主流で、我が家でも三段にまとめます。三が日、日持ちさせるために酢漬けや、味を濃くして保存が効くように調理します。一品は自分で作りたいものです。簡単に作れるおすすめは、千切り大根・人参を酢漬けした紅白なますと、鶏ひき肉を広げて焼くのし鶏。黒豆などは中をくり抜いたゆず釜に入れると、華やかで食材の仕切りにもなり便利です。

Festive Dishes for the New Year: Osechi is a celebratory meal cooked with the hope of a good harvest, of the safety of one's family, and of fertility and prosperity. Stuffing the dishes in lacquered boxes carries the auspicious meaning of "layering happiness." The basic style layers four boxes from the first layer up to fourth layer, with the dishes inside varying by region and household. The most common style is having three layered boxes, my home included. The first three days of the New Year are meant to give housewives a break from housework, so the dishes are pickled or heavily seasoned to preserve well.

かまぼこ Kamaboko
日の出を象徴するもので、紅は慶びを、白は神聖を表わしている。
Symbolizing "sunrise," the red represents celebration and the white represents sacredness.

紅白なます Kohaku-namasu
人参の紅は魔除け、大根の白は清浄を意味している酢漬け。
A pickled dish in which the carrot symbolizes the warding off of evil spirits, and the daikon radish symbolizes purity.

伊達巻き Date-maki
巻物にみたて知性を表わしている。「伊達」とは華やかという意味。
Resembling a scroll, this dish signifies intelligence. The word "date" means radiance.

昆布巻き Kobu-maki
よろこぶの語呂合わせから、一家発展の縁起物として。
A play on the word "yorokobu" (to be happy), it's believed to bring good luck.

田作り Tazukuri
五穀豊穣、稲の豊作を願う気持ちを表わしている。小さくても尾頭付き。
This dish represents the wish for a great rice harvest. Though small, it's served from head to tail.

きんとん Kinton
黄色は黄金の色、栗は小判にみたてて豊かな年を願う。
The yellow resembles gold while the chestnut looks like koban (oval gold coins) to wish for a prosperous year.

黒豆 Kuromame
年中、まめに働いて健康でいられるようにという願いを表わしている。
A pun on "mame" (diligence), it symbolizes staying healthy year round and working hard.

のし鶏 Noshidori
松風焼きともいう。おめでたい末広がりの羽子板型にする。
Also called matsukaze-yaki, it's prepared into a celebratory shape of a flared battledore.

数の子 Kazunoko
数の子はニシンの卵。卵の数が多いことから子孫繁栄を願う。
As it's made up of many eggs, this dish contains a wish to be gifted with fertility and prosperity.

煮しめ Nishime
野菜や鶏肉などを一つの鍋で一緒に煮ることから、家庭円満を願う。
Since this dish is prepared by simmering a colorful array of vegetables and chicken in one pot, it represents the safety of one's family.

73

| 季節のごはん | Seasonal Dishes

055 餅
Mochi

餅米を水に浸してから蒸して、杵で粒がなくなるまでなめらかにつきます。大昔から日本では、お祝いには欠かせない縁起物の食材。おもに関東では角餅、関西では丸餅の形にします。お正月の鏡餅は丸い餅を2つ重ねることで、円満に年を重ねることを願ってきました。

Rice Cake: Mochi is made by soaking glutinous sweet rice in water before steaming, then smoothly pounding it with a pestle until the grains are gone. Japan has long observed the tradition of believing in the divinity of rice production; any celebratory day such as New Year's Day calls for this essential ingredient that is said to bring good luck. Generally, the Kanto region uses squared mochi while the Kansai region uses round mochi.

磯辺巻き Isobe-maki
切り餅を焼き、熱いうちに醤油をつけて海苔を巻いたもの。
Made by grilling kiri mochi (pre-cut mochi), and pouring soy sauce while it's hot and wrapping it in nori seaweed.

あんころ餅 Ankoro Mochi
やわらかい餅をあんでからめたもの。
Made with freshly pounded mochi tossed in red bean paste.

安倍川餅 Abekawa Mochi
やわらかい餅にきなこと白砂糖をまぶしたもの。
Prepared by tossing freshly pounded mochi in kinako (roasted soy bean flour), then garnishing it with white sugar.

からみ餅 Karami Mochi
やわらかい餅を醤油入りの大根おろしでからめたもの。
Freshly pounded mochi tossed in grated daikon with soy sauce.

056 雑煮
Zoni

新年に神様に供えたお餅を他の食材と一緒に煮て、神様と一緒のものを頂くことで、力が授かると考えられていたのが由来とも。正月三が日には欠くことのできない一品です。お雑煮は地方色がとても豊かで、お餅の形、使う具材や味つけは多彩で、たとえば、関東は醤油味、関西は白味噌で仕上げます。我が家は東京流で、鶏だしに、焼き餅、なるとと三つ葉に、醤油と塩だけのシンプルな飽きのこない味に仕立てます。

Rice Cake and Vegetables Soup: Zoni derives from the belief that, by simmering the mochi served to god in the New Year together with other ingredients and thereby eating the same thing as god, people would receive divine power. It's an essential dish for the first three days of the New Year, eaten to appreciate the previous year's harvest and people's health while praying for the New Year's rich harvest and safety of one's family. The mochi shape, ingredients, and dashi stock vary by region; in the Kanto region the mochi is flavored with soy sauce while it's flavored with white miso in the Kansai region. **Recipe➡P.157**

| 季節のごはん | Seasonal Dishes

2月3日 節分
Setsubun

February 3

Setsubun means "seasonal division." Under the nijushi-sekki, the Lunar calendar system with 24 seasonal divisions that expressed the subtle changes in the four seasons, risshun was considered a marker of the new year when winter ended and spring began. Setsubun, the day before risshun, has long been cherished like New Year's Eve.

節分は季節の分かれ目という意味。古来より四季の微妙な変化を表現した「二十四節気」では立春・立夏・立秋・立冬の前日をすべて節分と呼んでいました。「立春」で冬が終わり、また一年が始まると考えられ、立春の前日の節分は春のくる嬉びを感じる行事で大晦日のように大切にされてきました。豆まきをして古い年の嫌なことを追い払い、春とともに福を呼び込みましょう。

057 福豆
Fukumame

節分の日は「鬼は外、福は内」といいながら豆をまき、邪気を払います。福を呼び込むので福豆。豆をまき終えたら、自分の歳より一つ多い数だけ豆を食べ、無病息災を願います。

On the day of Setsubun, the custom is to throw these roasted soybeans while saying "Demons out! Luck in!" to drive away the evil spirits. They are called fukumame since they bring fuku (luck and happiness). You eat the number of beans of your age to pray for a safe year.

058 恵方巻き
Eho-maki

その年のおめでたいとされる方角を向き、無言で一気に丸かじりする恵方巻きはいつからか全国区に。鬼のこん棒を模している巻き物なので、具材をたくさん入れ、できるだけ太く作ります。

This is a thick sushi roll that people eat up in silence while facing the direction of eho (the direction that is said to bring good luck that year.)

| Seasonal Dishes

【3月3日】
ひな祭り
Hinamatsuri

桃の節句ともいわれ、ひな人形や桃の花を飾り、
女の子の健やかな成長と幸せを願って、祝う行事です。
各地に伝統的なひな飾りがあり、祝い方も地域や家庭によって違います。
内裏びなの飾り方は、向かって左が男びな、右が女びなが一般的ですが、
関西では逆に飾るところがあるようです。
我が家では十日間くらいひな人形を飾り、3月3日が終わるとしまっています。
節句が終わりひな人形を片づけないでいると、
お嫁に行き遅れるという迷信もあります。

Girl's Day, March 3
Also called Momo-no-Sekku (Peach Blossom Festival), Hinamatsuri is an event to pray for and celebrate the growth and happiness of girls. Various areas have their own traditional doll decorations and celebration customs. The emperor and empress dolls are placed to the left and right respectively but some parts of the Kansai region ornament the opposite way. I usually display my hina dolls 10 days before March 3 and take them down right away, since leaving them out after the celebration is said to lead to a late marriage for the daughter.

059 ちらし寿司
Chirashi-zushi

平安時代には海老と菜の花のなれ寿司で祝ったそうです。私は酢飯を甘めにし、海と山の幸をたっぷりと盛りつけます。春の旬を彩りよく飾る、ひな祭りを祝う華やかで代表的な料理です。

Scattered Topping Sushi: A colorful signature dish to celebrate Hinamatsuri, it's vinegared sushi rice topped with seasonal ocean and mountain fare.

060 潮汁
Ushio-jiru

はまぐりの澄まし汁。対の貝殻には「よい人と出会えますよう」と願う意味が込められています。

Clear Clam Soup: In this clear clam soup, the paired up shells symbolize a wish to meet somebody special.

061 桜餅
Sakura Mochi

蒸した餅米や薄皮で小豆あんを包み、塩漬けした桜の葉を巻いた春の生菓子です。

Mochi with Cherry Leaves: A fresh spring sweet, it is red bean paste wrapped in steamed glutinous rice or thin dough, then covered in salted cherry leaves.

79

季節のごはん | Seasonal Dishes

Cherry-Blossom Viewing

An essential spring custom in Japan since the Heian period, Ohanami is when everyone gathers for feasts under the cherry trees in full bloom, to eat, drink, and relish in the beauty of the cherry blossoms. Even your typical rolled sushi or inari sushi can heighten the celebratory feel when served in a jubako (multi-tiered lacquered box).

お花見
Ohanami

満開の桜の木の下でごちそうを囲み、桜の花の美しさを楽しむ——平安の昔から行なわれてきた日本の春の欠かせない風習です。昔から春の野遊びにはお酒とごちそうがつきもの。いつもの巻き寿司やいなり寿司もお重に詰めるとよそ行きの顔になり、華やぎも楽しさもアップしますね。

80

062 三色団子
Sanshoku-dango

桜の赤、野草の緑、白は早春の空、または人を表わしたといわれる三色団子。お花見の時に食べるのが広まったのは江戸時代ということです。

Tricolor Rice Dumplings: The pink represents cherry blossom and the green stands for wild grass while many theories remain for the meaning of the white color. Either way, this tricolor dango is said to depict the early spring sky.

063 巻き寿司
Maki-zushi

切り口の彩りを考えて、桜色のデンブを入れ、お花見の太巻きを作ります。具はできるだけ重ねるように並べると、巻き上がりがきれいになります。

Rolled Sushi: Since this dish uses all kinds of fillings for the rolls and adds a colorful touch when sliced, it's a popular type of sushi for events like picnics and field trips.

064 いなり寿司
Inari-zushi

農耕の神様、稲荷神に捧げるお供えが由来。湯がいた揚げを醤油、砂糖、だしを入れた漬け汁に一晩寝かせるだけ。煮込まないのでやさしい味に仕上がります。

Sushi Wrapped in Fried Tofu: Vinegared sushi rice stuffed inside sweetly simmered abura-age (deep-fried tofu pouches). It's believed to have been an offering to the Shinto god Inari, the god of agriculture. **Recipe➡P.157**

季節のごはん | Seasonal Dishes

Children's Day, May 5

Children's Day celebrates the healthy growth and future success of boys. Families fly koinobori (carp-shaped streamers) outside and decorate their houses with items like armor, helmets, and warrior dolls. It originates from a Chinese custom of driving away evil spirits with irises. After the second war, this day was designated as a national holiday and renamed "Children's Day."

【5月5日】
端午の節句
Tango no Sekku

男の子の健やかな成長と立身出世を願って祝う行事です。鯉のぼりを空に泳がせ、鎧兜や武者人形を飾ります。もともとは菖蒲で邪気をはらう中国の風習からきたもの。戦後、「子どもの日」として祝日になりました。

065 柏餅
Kashiwa Mochi

上新粉を蒸してあんをはさんで、柏の葉で包んだもの。柏は葉が落ちないので、家系が絶えないという縁起のよい木といわれています。
Steamed joshinko (rice flour) filled with sweet bean paste and wrapped in oak leaves. The Oak tree is considered an auspicious tree that continues the family line.

066 ちまき
Chimaki

餅米を笹の葉でつつみ、伊草で縛って蒸した和菓子。もともと中国から伝えられたもので、厄払いの意味が込められているそうです。
A Japanese sweet that consists of glutinous rice wrapped in bamboo leaves, tied with a common rush, and steamed. It originated in China as a food to fend off evil spirits.

067 筍ごはん
Takenoko Gohan

筍のようにまっすぐ、すくすくと成長するようにと、端午の節句には欠かせない縁起もの。薄味にして炊き、筍の香りを引き立てます。
Bamboo Rice: A type of seasonal mixed rice, it's the essential spring ingredient bamboo cooked together with seasoning.

季節のごはん　Seasonal Dishes

土用
Doyo

土用は年に四回ある季節のかわり目、
立夏、立秋、立冬、立春の前18日間を指します。
江戸時代には、特に立秋前の丑の日を重視し、
夏バテをしないようにと薬草風呂に入ったり、
「う」のつくウリや鰻、梅干などを食べる風習もありました。
土用の鰻は蘭学者の平賀源内が夏にお客が減ってしまう鰻屋のために、
一計を案じて広めたといわれています。

Dog Days of Summer

Originally, doyo took place four times a year at the change of each season. Nowadays only the "summer doyo" remains. The custom is to eat unagi (eel) on this Midsummer Day to prevent summer heat fatigue.

068 鰻重
Una-ju

鰻の蒲焼きは関東では背開き、関西では腹開きと、さばき方が正反対。焼き方も異なり、関西流は蒸しません。

Kabayaki is a barbequed eel filet with a sweet soy sauce over rice. In the Kanto region the eel is split open along the back while in the Kansai region, it's split along the belly. The grilling methods completely differ between the two regions. This dish is gaining popularity all over the world.

| 季節のごはん | Seasonal Dishes

お彼岸
Ohigan

昼と夜の長さが同じになる春分と秋分の日の
前後3日間ずつ、合計7日間のことをお彼岸と呼びます。
日本独特のご先祖さまを供養する仏教行事です。
「彼岸」とは仏教用語で、
この世を離れて仏の世界（むこう岸）に行く
という意味だそうです。
亡くなった人に思いをはせ、
お墓参りに行ったり、おはぎを作って供えます。

Ohigan refers to the two equinoctial weeks during the year, in spring (Vernal Equinox Day) and autumn (Autumnal Equinox Day), when the length of day and night become approximately equivalent. For this Buddhist event that commemorates ancestors, people visit their family's graves to pray for the departed souls and prepare ohagi as offerings.

069 おはぎ
Ohagi

餅米を蒸して団子にしてあんで包みます。春は牡丹の花にちなんでぼた餅、秋は萩の花にちなんでおはぎと呼びます。あんの他に、きな粉と胡麻をまぶして三色仕立てに。

A sweet consisting of steamed glutinous rice rolled into dango (rice dumplings) shapes and wrapped in red bean paste. In the spring it may be called botamochi, and in the autumn called ohagi.

Seasonal Dishes

十五夜
Jugoya

一年の中でも特に空気が澄み、月が美しく見えるという十五夜にでる満月を「中秋の名月」といい、昔から秋の収穫を祝い、お月見をする風習があります。月を表わす月見団子と、魔除けの力があるといわれるススキの穂を飾り、秋の収穫を供え、実りに感謝する行事です。

Full Moon Festival
The full moon that appears on Jugoya (August 15 of the Lunar calendar) when the air is considered especially fresh is called chushu-no-meigetsu (harvest of moon). The ancient custom involves celebrating the fall harvest and practicing otsukimi (moon-viewing). For this event, people decorate with susuki (Japanese pampas grass that's believed to ward off evil spirits), and offer tsukimi-dango ("moon" rice dumplings) and the fall harvest to show appreciation for the fruitful year.

070 月見団子
Tsukimi Dango

十五夜にちなんで団子の数は15個、または月数の12個を三方にのせます。お月様にお供えするものなので、月が見えるところや床の間に。

Full Moon Rice Dumplings: Since Jugoya means the 15th night, 15 dumplings, or 12 for the number of months, are stacked on top of a sanpo (a small stand used in Shinto rituals to present offerings) as decoration.

季節のごはん | Seasonal Dishes

【 12月31日 】

大晦日

Oomisoka

昔は月の終わりを晦日といったことから、
一年最後の日に「大」をつけて大晦日となったといいます。
お正月の準備や大掃除で忙しい一日が終わったら、
年越しそばを食べるのが最後の締めくくりです。
食べるタイミングは家庭によって様々ですが、
我が家では年をまたぐと縁起が悪いので、
除夜の鐘の前に食べ終わるようにします。

New Year's Eve, December 31
Since the last day of the month was traditionally called
misoka, the last day of the year became Oomisoka, with
the 'oo' meaning big. After a busy day of preparing for
New Year's Day and thoroughly cleaning the house, the
final wrap-up involves eating toshikoshi soba. Superstition
says it's bad luck to drag it into the New Year so most
households finish the dish before the bell of New Year's
Eve.

071 年越し蕎麦
Toshikoshi Soba

蕎麦は切れやすいことから「今年一年の厄を断ち切る」という意味があり、縁起をかついで食されるようになったとか。江戸時代に広まったといわれています。ちなみに食べ残すと金運を逃すといわれるので、食べ切れる量を準備しましょう。

This noodle dish is eaten on New Year's Eve to bring good luck in the next year. Since cooked soba breaks off easily, this custom seems to carry the meaning of "cutting off bad luck and omens from this year."

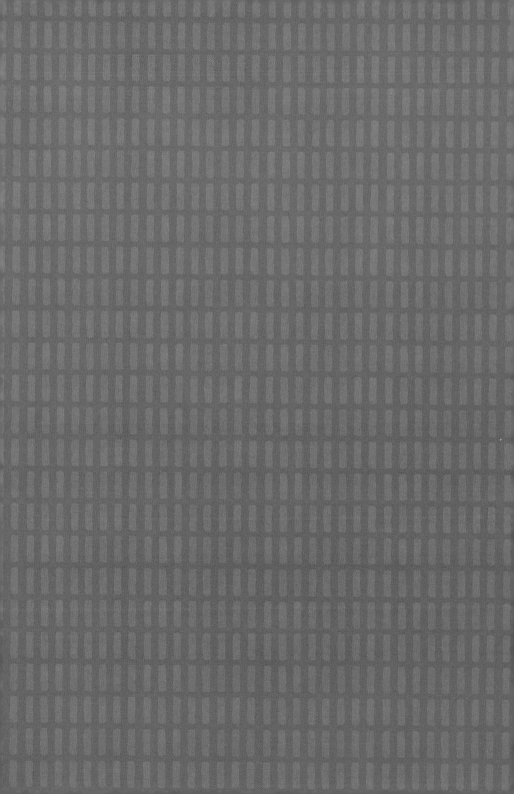

いつもの飲みもの

Everyday Drinks

| いつもの飲みもの | Everyday Drinks

072 日本茶
Nihon-cha

緑茶の代表格といえば煎茶。煎茶の持つ特徴「甘み」「渋み」「苦み」は、そのいれ方で味わうことができます。茶葉は1人分2gくらいを目安に。ポイントはお湯の温度で、熱湯を湯のみに移すと10℃下がることを知っていると便利です。最初は低い温度から入れるのが基本で、70℃くらいで「甘み」を楽しみ、二煎目は少し高めの80℃で「渋み」を。三煎目は90℃以上のお湯を入れて最後に「苦み」を味わいます。

Japanese Tea: Green tea is the most typically consumed Japanese tea. Knowing the green tea characteristics of sweetness (amami), astringency (shibumi), and bitterness (nigami) will help you brew a delicious pot of tea. Use about 2 grams of tea leaves per person. The water temperature is key. For the first steeping, enjoy the sweetness with the water temperature at 70℃. Keep in mind that pouring the boiling water into the teacup decreases the temperature by 10℃. For the second steeping, increase the temperature to 80℃ to enjoy the astringency. For the third steeping, pour hot water over 90℃ to savor the bitterness. And now you know the secret to brewing delicious green tea.

いろいろなお茶　Various Types of Nihon-cha

煎茶
Sen-cha

生葉を蒸す、煎るなど熱処理をして作られる。すっきりとした味わいで最も一般的な緑茶の種類。

Green Tea: Preparing green tea involves heat treatment such as steaming or roasting the leaves. Known for its clean taste, it's one of the most commonly consumed green teas.

ほうじ茶
Hoji-cha

煎茶を煎ったほうじ茶は、香りを楽しむお茶。熱湯を注いで30秒くらい蒸らす。低カフェイン。

Roasted Green Tea: This is roasted sen-cha, and it's all about enjoying the tea aroma. Pour the boiling water and brew for about 30 seconds. It contains less caffeine.

玄米茶
Genmai-cha

炒り玄米をメインに煎茶、番茶をブレンドしたもの。緑茶に比べてカフェインが少ない。

Brown Rice Tea: A blend of mainly roasted brown rice with some sen-cha and ban-cha, contains less caffeine.

麦茶
Mugi-cha

大麦を焙煎したもので、ミネラルが豊富。身体のほてりを下げる働きがある。夏場に冷やして飲む。

Barley Tea: Made by roasting barley, this tea has a high nutritional value. It's typically consumed as a cold drink in the summer.

| いつもの飲みもの | Everyday Drinks

073 抹茶
Matcha

てん茶という普通の緑茶とは違う方法で育てられた茶葉を蒸し、乾燥させてから茶臼でひいたのが抹茶。甘みと苦さを味わう、日本の伝統文化である茶道で使うお茶です。茶葉を丸ごと飲む抹茶はカテキンの健康効果もあり、巷では抹茶ダイエットとして人気を呼ぶほどで、いまや日本のスーパーフードとして世界でも注目を集めています。私はお菓子作りだけでなく、ドレッシングやパスタソースにも取り入れています。

This tea is made from tencha, grown differently than regular green tea. It is steamed, dried, and ground with a stone mill. More expensive than regular tea, it's used for traditional tea ceremony (sado) to enjoy the sweetness and bitterness. The health benefits of catechins has helped matcha attract attention as Japan's superfood. Make matcha regularly to incorporate it into your daily routine.

抹茶の点て方 How to Make Matcha

❶ あらかじめ熱湯を入れてお茶碗を温め、お湯をすてる。茶碗に茶杓で2杯の抹茶を入れる。
Warm the tea bowl by pouring boiling water in advance, then pour it out. Put 2 teaspoons of matcha into the tea bowl.

❷ 一度沸騰したお湯に水を入れ落ちつかせ、80℃前後にお湯を冷ます。そのお湯をゆっくりと注ぐ。
Boil the water to remove the chlorine smell, then cool the water temperature to around 80℃. Slowly pour into the tea bowl.

❸ 最初は底の抹茶を分散させるようにゆっくりと混ぜ、茶筅を底からあげて、手首を前後に振って一気に点てる。
Slowly whisk to disperse the matcha at the bottom of the tea bowl, then lift the bamboo whisk from the bottom, and move your wrist back and forth quickiy to whisk.

❹ 中央に泡が盛り上がるように、ゆっくりと静かに茶筅を持ち上げて出来上がり。細かい泡が抹茶の味を引き立てる。
To finish off, slowly lift up the bamboo whisk to gather the bubbles in the middle.

いつもの飲みもの | Everyday Drinks

074 日本酒
Nihonshu

世界でも人気の日本酒。白米を蒸して麹と水を加えて発酵・熟成させる日本特有の製法で醸造されます。原料や精米歩合により、本醸造酒・純米酒・吟醸酒に分類されます。全国には1600以上の蔵元があり、美味しい水と米が、香り豊かな酒を生み出す決め手に。また、飲む温度によって味わいが大きく変わるのも特長です。吟醸酒の華やかな香りは冷酒で引き立ち、アミノ酸の旨みは熱燗で味わえます。

Japanese Sake: Popular around the world, Japanese sake is brewed through a unique process of steaming white rice with koji (essential food culture for making miso and sake) and water, then fermenting and aging. Depending on the ingredients or polishing ratio, it is categorized into "honjozo-shu," "junmai-shu," and "ginjo-shu." Japan contains more than 1,600 sake breweries. Fragrant and delicious sake relies on fresh water and quality rice. Served chilled (reishu), heated (atsukan), or luke warm (nurukan), it offers an assortment of ways to drink and enjoy the taste.

075 焼酎
Shochu

長い歴史を持つ日本独自の蒸留酒の焼酎。芋、米、麦、黒糖、蕎麦などで作られている焼酎ですが、栗、しそ、胡麻、山芋、牛乳など珍しい原料もあります。日本酒よりも焼酎のほうが生産・消費ともに多いということです。日本酒に比べると世界であまり知られていなかった焼酎も、カクテルで飲むのが広まり、人気に火がつきはじめています。焼酎の良さは自分の好みの飲み方ができるところで、私は食後酒として黒糖焼酎をロックで飲むのが好きです。

Whether it's from potato, rice, wheat, brown sugar, or buckwheat, this liquor is produced all over Japan from an array of ingredients. It's a spirit unique to Japan with a long history, and produced and consumed even more than Japanese sake. Although not as common outside of Japan, drinking shochu cocktail-style has become popular. Whether it's served as a chuhai (shochu with soda and juice), on the rocks, or mixed with hot water, fragrant and flavorful shochu matches with any seasonal meal and style.

いつもの飲みもの | Everyday Drinks

076 ビール
Biru

ビールは基本的に酵母の違いでラガーとエールに分けられます。ラガーはすっきりとした喉ごしがいいタイプで、アジアで好まれて飲まれるそうです。エールはパンチのある香り豊かなタイプで、コクがあるのが特徴です。

Beer: Depending on the type of yeast, beer is categorized into lager and ale. Craftsmen in small breweries carefully produce craft beer, which is gaining popularity. To this day, however draft beer reigns supreme in Japan.

077 酎ハイ
Chuhai

焼酎の酎と炭酸で割るハイボールで「酎ハイ」。アルコール度数が低いので、気楽に飲める日本発祥の人気カクテルです。焼酎の割材として梅やぶどう風味のシロップを加えた酎ハイの原型は戦前からあったそう。

Chuhai is a highball drink mixing shochu with soda. Served at izakayas and widely consumed, its versatility lies in adding various mixers like fruit juice, fruits, matcha or sour plum shiso.

078 ワイン
Wain

はじめて日本産ワインが製造、産業化されたのが約150年前。最近では輸出量が増え、世界のワインコンクールで上位を占めるように。赤白ともに果実の香りの高さ、甘みが日本産の特徴だといわれています。

Wine: Japan's wine consumption continues to increase as it has taken root. Perhaps owing to the health benefits of polyphenols, red wine is especially popular. Although associated with Western food, it perfectly suits Japanese food as well.

079 梅酒
Umeshu

昔は、6月に梅が出回ると、多くの家で梅酒作りが始まりました。梅と氷砂糖と焼酎というシンプルさ。新しい梅酒を仕込む時に、去年の梅酒も飲み頃になっていますが、年代ものの梅酒はまるでブランディーのような味わいです。

Plum Sake: Traditionally, when plums would hit the market around June, many households would make their own plum sake from a simple recipe of plum, crystal sugar, and shochu. It will be ready to be served a year later, while preparing the next batch. It's delicious served on the rocks or as a highball.

和のお菓子
Japanese Sweets

和のお菓子 | Japanese Sweets

080 生菓子
Namagashi

日本の伝統的なお菓子、和菓子が甘くなったのは茶道が始まった室町時代になってからだといいます。奈良時代に唐から入ってきた黒砂糖は、まだその頃は薬と考えられていました。草餅など古来の餅菓子は植物から甘みをとっていたそうです。そして、江戸時代に寒天の発見で練り羊羹が生まれ、美しく雅な京菓子に発展しました。季節の行事に合わせたものや、自然の風物をかたどったもの、旬の素材を使い、その季節だけに作られるもの。昔から、四季折々を大事にしてきた日本ならではの知恵がつまったのが、和菓子の特長です。和菓子は脂肪分をほとんど含まないので、実は低カロリーでヘルシーなものです。

Fresh Japanese Confections: Traditional confections became sweeter when tea

大福 Daifuku
薄くのばした餅であんを包んだもの。苺を包む苺大福も人気。
Literally meaning "good luck," daifuku is thin mochi stuffed with sweet bean paste. Strawberry daifuku is also popular.

きんつば Kintsuba
寒天で固めた粒あん生地に、水溶きした小麦粉をつけて焼いたもの。
Tsubu-an (chunky azuki bean paste) dough set with kanten (Japanese agar) and wrapped in flour is mixed with water, then grilled.

草餅 Kusa Mochi
ヨモギを練り込んだ餅の中に、あんを入れて丸めた春らしい和菓子。
A vernal Japanese confection, made from mochi kneaded with mugwort that's filled with sweet bean paste and rolled up.

饅頭 Manju
上用粉や米粉、小麦粉などの生地であんを包み、蒸して仕上げる。
Dough made from ingredients such as glutinous rice flour, rice flour, and wheat flour that's filled with sweet bean paste and steamed to serve.

最中 Monaka
餅米の粉を蒸して焼いた種皮に、水飴の入ったあんをはさんだもの。
Sweet bean jam filling sandwiched between wafers made from steaming and grilling glutinous rice powder.

生八つ橋 Nama Yatsuhashi
米粉にシナモンや砂糖を練りこんだ生地であんをはさむ、京都の菓子。
A famous Japanese sweet from Kyoto made from rice-flour based dough kneaded with cinnamon and sugar and filled with sweet bean paste.

ceremonies started in the Muromachi period. Black sugar was considered medicinal when it first arrived from China in the Nara period. Whether these sweets are tailored to seasonal events and natural sceneries, or made exclusively when seasonal ingredients are available, only a country like Japan that has traditionally cherished the four seasons could serve such confections. Containing very little fat, they actually make for great, healthy sweets.

くず餅 Kuzumochi
小麦粉のでん.ぷんを発酵させて作る関東風とくず粉を使う関西風がある。
The Kanto (Eastern Japan) style uses starch from wheat flour while the Kansai (Western Japan) style uses kuzuko (kudzu starch).

栗かのこ Kuri Kanoko
栗と砂糖のみで作るきんとん菓子。丸のままの栗に栗あんがからめてある。
A sweet bean paste ball decorated with colorful crumbled pieces of sweet bean paste varying throughout the seasons.

羊羹 Yokan
小豆を煮て寒天液を入れ、火にかけながら練り上げ、型で固めたもの。
Kanten (Japanese agar) added to cooked azuki beans that's kneaded and heated, then poured into a mold to set firm.

栗饅頭 Kuri Manju
中の白あんや栗あんを皮で包み、表面に卵黄を塗りツヤよく焼いたもの。
White bean paste or chestnut paste filling wrapped and coated with egg yolk for a glossy finish.

カステラ Kasutera
卵を泡立て、砂糖・小麦粉・牛乳を混ぜて焼く南蛮菓子。
A baked sweet made from whipped eggs, sugar, flour, and milk that was brought to Japan from Portugal.

練り切り Nerikiri
白あんに求肥を練り込み、色をつけて繊細な四季を表現する上生菓子。
A fresh sweet made from kneading gyuhi (soft mocha) in sweet white bean paste that uses color to express the seasons.

| 和のお菓子 | Japanese Sweets

Shiruko

Anmitsu

Zenzai

081 あんみつ
Anmitsu

塩ゆでした赤えんどう豆、寒天、フルーツなどの具材にあんを添えて、蜜をかける和風デザート。生クリームやアイスクリームを加えたものもあります。

A Japanese desert that consists of ingredients such as red peas boiled in salt water, kanten (Japanese agar), and fruits served with sweet bean paste and honey. It may also be served with whipped cream or ice cream.

082 汁粉
Shiruko

小豆を砂糖で甘く煮た小豆汁の中に、お餅や白玉団子を入れたものです。関東ではこしあんを使うと御前汁粉、粒あんを使うと田舎汁粉といい、関西ではこしあんのものを汁粉といいます。

Cook azuki beans with sugar to make azuki porridge, then add mochi, shiratama dango (sweet mochi dumplings), or candied chestnuts. It's called gozen-shiruko when using koshi-an (strained bean paste) and inaka-shiruko when using tsubu-an (crunchy bean paste.)

083 ぜんざい
Zenzai

関西では粒あんの汁粉をぜんざいといい、関東では汁気の少ない粒あんの汁ものです。焼いた餅や白玉を添えます。意外と美味しいのが夏の冷しぜんざい。白玉団子のツルリとしたノドごしの良さが涼しさをよびます。

Zenzai seems to differ between Kanto (Eastern Japan) and Kansai (Western Japan). The Kanto style uses tsubu-an (crunchy bean paste), which is less watery, and adds grilled mochi or shiratama (sweet mochi dumplings.)

和のお菓子 | Japanese Sweets

084 どら焼き
Dorayaki

小麦粉・砂糖・卵を混ぜた生地を焼き、あんをはさんだ、家庭でも簡単に作れるお菓子です。関西では奈良の三笠山に見たてて三笠ともいわれています。

Red Bean Pancake: Dorayaki is a sweet consisting of flour, sugar, and eggs mixed into a batter and baked into two fluffy round patties that are filled with red bean paste. In the Kansai region, it is also called Mikasa from Mount Mikasa in Nara. **Recipe➡P.157**

108

たい焼き
Taiyaki

明治時代に縁起物の鯛を型どり、売り出した「浪花家総本店」が始まりだそうです。焼きたての熱々を頂くのが美味しく、並んでも食べたいお店がいくつかあります。表面がカリッと焼かれているものが好きです。

Taiyaki is a baked snack made from flour-based batter poured into a sea-bream-shaped mold and filled with red bean paste called an. It's most delicious when freshly baked; many popular shops have quite the wait.

かき氷
Kakigori

かき氷といえば、海の家を思い出します。最近は天然氷を使ったかき氷が大人気ですね。天然水の氷は透明で固く、薄く削ることができるので、空気を含んでフワフワのかき氷に仕上がるそうです。

Kakigori is a summer tradition, the most popular ones using natural ice. The most famous Japanese style uses matcha, red beans, and condensed milk, topped with shiratama (sweet mochi dumplings.)

| 和のお菓子 | Japanese Sweets |

087 干菓子
Higashi

水分の少ない乾いたお菓子のことを干菓子といいます。大きく分類すると、焼いて作る焼き物の煎餅類、煎って作る煎り物のおこし、型に入れて固める押し物の落雁、熱を加え糖蜜をかけて作る掛け物の金平糖などに分けられます。生菓子に比べると、日持ちもよく手軽におやつにつまめる、いつもの和菓子です。由来をみると、ボウロや金平糖、色鮮やかな有平糖などは、南蛮菓子といわれ、室町時代にポルトガルやスペインから入って日本風になり、和菓子の仲間になったものなのです。お茶席などにも出される京干菓子は種類も多く、京都には有名な老舗のお店がたくさんあります。

Dry Confections: Higashi refers to dry sweets containing little moisture. Broadly categorized they include senbei, which is baked or grilled,

せんべい Senbei
うるち米の粉をこねて蒸し、薄く型抜きし、醤油をつけて焼いたもの。
Kneaded and steamed uruchi-mai (non-glutinous rice) flour that's thinly shaped in a mold, then dried and baked or grilled with soy sauce.

らくがん Rakugan
米のでんぷんに水飴を混ぜ、型に入れ乾燥させたもの。日本三大銘菓。
A sweet made from rice starch mixed with syrup that's poured in a mold and dried, it's considered one of the three greatest Japanese confections.

和三盆 Wasambon
サトウキビで作る四国の伝統菓子。砂糖を三度盆の上で研ぐことが由来。
A sugarcane sweet from Shikoku. The name means "three trays," referring to the process of hand-kneading the sugar three times on trays.

あられ Arare
餅米からできているので、うるち米で作る煎餅とは違い、軽い食感。
Made from glutinous rice, it differs from senbei, which is made from non-glutinous rice. Serve as a perfect light snack.

甘納豆 Amanatto
豆を砂糖と共に煮詰め、さらに砂糖をまぶしたもの。
Beans boiled with sugar and further candied.

金平糖 Kompeito
ザラメなどに糖蜜をかけ熱し、長時間かけて回転させながら突起を作る。
Small lumps of starch made by heating the core of granulated sugar while coating with syrup.

110

okoshi, which is roasted, rakugan, which is pressed and molded, and konpeito, which is heated and coated. Compared to fresh confections, they last longer and serve as casual snacks. Originally, the likes of boro and konpeito were called nanban-gashi (European sweets) since they were imported from Portugal and Spain in the Muromachi period before transforming into Japanese sweets. Among these, Kyoto sweets have many variations including those used in tea ceremonies; the city is filled with famous, long-established confectionery shops.

ボウロ Boro
小麦粉に卵・砂糖などを加え型に抜いて焼いたポルトガル伝来の固い菓子。
Biscuits imported from Portugal, boro is made by adding egg and sugar in flour, cutting out the shapes and baking.

干し柿 Hoshi-gaki
渋柿の皮をむいて干し、甘みを出した日本の昔からのドライフルーツ。
A Japanese dry fruit that's peeled skin of shibugaki (astringent persimmons) dried to bring out the sweetness.

かりんとう Karinto
小麦粉の生地を棒状にし、揚げて黒蜜をからめて乾燥させたもの。
Flour dough rolled into long sticks that's fried, dressed with dark molasses, and dried for a crunchy and sweet taste.

おこし Okoshi
米などの穀物を細かく挽いて練り合わせ、水飴で固めた堅い菓子。
A crunchy sweet made from finely grounded grains like rice that's kneaded and held together with starch syrup.

八つ橋 Yatsuhashi
京都を代表する和菓子。シナモンの香りと琴の形を模しているのが特徴。
Dough made from rice flour, sugar, and cinnamon, is thinly stretched into koto (Japanese zither) shapes and baked.

金太郎飴 Kintaro-ame
水飴と砂糖でのばして作る、棒状の飴。どこを切っても顔が現れる飴細工。
Made from stretched out sugar and starch syrup, this cylinder-shaped candy shows the face of Kintaro or "Golden Boy," a folklore hero.

| 和のお菓子 | Japanese Sweets |

088 わらび餅
Warabi Mochi

わらびの地下茎から取れるデンプン・水・砂糖で作る和菓子。くず餅に似ていますが原料が違います。きなこや黒蜜の替わりにココアをまぶすのもひと味違って美味しいです。
A Japanese sweet made from starch derived from warabi (bracken) rhizome, water, and sugar. Although resembling kuzu-mochi, it is made from a different type of starch. Serve with kinako (roasted soy bean flour) and kuromitsu (black sugar syrup).

Warabi Mochi

Kuzukiri

Tokoroten

089 くずきり
Kuzukiri

くず粉を水に溶かし、型に入れて加熱し固めたものを細長く切ったものです。くず粉は体を温めてくれる力と整腸作用があり、下痢や風邪の時におすすめです。
To make kuzukiri, kuzuko (kudzu starch) is dissolved in water, shaped in a mold, heated, set, and thinly sliced into noodle shapes. Hailing from Kyoto, this sweet dish cools the hot summers with its slick texture.

090 ところてん
Tokoroten

テングサなどの海藻類と水だけで作られたところてんは、食物繊維が豊富で低カロリー。ダイエット中にはおすすめのおやつ。酢醤油や辛子をつけて頂きますが、関西では黒みつをかける人もいるようです。
To make tokoroten, seaweeds such as tengusa (a type of red seaweed) are soaked in water, boiled, and dissolved. Then it's shaped into a mold, chilled, set, and finally pressed against a tokoroten device to create thin noodle shapes. Serve with vinegar-soy sauce and mustard.

和の材
Japanese Ingredients

Japanese Ingredients

091 醤油
Shoyu

いわずと知れた日本の伝統的な発酵調味料。ルーツは古代中国の醤が起源だといわれています。日本では野菜、海藻を材料とした草醤、魚の魚醤、穀物の穀醤などが縄文時代にあったそうです。それらが発展し、室町時代に今の醤油のようになったといわれています。甘い、酸っぱい、塩っぱい、苦い、そして旨みの5原味がそろっている優れた調味料です。蒸した大豆と炒った小麦、塩、麹菌の原材料を、発酵・熟成させてもろみを作ります。そのもろみから抽出したものが醤油で、発酵時間を長くすると色の濃い醤油ができます。白から溜まり醤油まで、色の濃度、香り、味のバランスも様々で、奥が深い醤油の世界です。最近は、卵かけごはん、お刺身、お肉など、素材をより美味しくする用途別のこだわり醤油が登場しています。

Soy Sauce: Whether it's used for dipping, drizzling, or seasoning, this traditional

濃口 Koikuchi
一般的によく使われている醤油。色、香りが豊かなので、特に煮物などこっくりとした色を出したい料理に向いている。
Generally the most popular soy sauce, it has a rich aroma and color, which is suitable for the browning seen in simmered dishes.

薄口 Usukuhci
関西で多く使われる醤油。淡口醤油ともいう。塩を多く使い発酵・熟成をゆるやかにする。素材の色を活かす料理に向いている。
Light soy sauce used frequently in the Kansai region, it contains a lot of salt, which slows down the fermentation and aging process and prevents the color from darkening. It is suitable for maintaining the ingredients' color when cooking.

白 Shiro
愛知発祥の一番色の薄い醤油。主原料は小麦で、大豆を少量混ぜて作られる。主に調理に使われる。
Originating in Aichi prefecture, it is made mainly with wheat and a smaller amount of soybeans. As the most light-colored soy sauce, it's used for cooking.

fermented seasoning forms the very foundation of Japanese cooking. Originating in an ancient Chinese sauce called hishio, it was perfected into the current form in the Muromachi period. It's an excellent seasoning that contains the five basic tastes of sweetness, sourness, saltiness, bitterness, and umami. Fermenting and maturing the raw ingredients of steamed soybean, roasted wheat, salt, and koji-kin (koji mold) produces moromi; soy sauce is what is extracted from this moromi. Lengthening the fermentation time produces darker soy sauce. Variations range from white soy sauce to tamari, each kind offering a different thickness, aroma, and flavor. Gourmet soy sauce has been recently appearing on the market such as those exclusively tailored to egg raw over rice, sashimi, or meat.

溜まり Tamari
愛知など中部地方で使われる濃厚な醤油。ほとんど大豆のみで作られるが、色のわりには甘みが強い。
A thick and rich soy sauce used in the central Chubu region such as Aichi. Although made almost entirely of soybeans, it has quite the sweet flavor for its color.

ポン酢 Ponzu
柑橘果汁に酢や醤油を入れて作られた調味料。鍋や焼き物などに使うことが多い。ドレッシングとしてもそのまま使える。
A soy sauce based condiment, made with citrus fruits and vinegar and used for one-pot meals or grilled food.

魚醤 Gyosho
魚を塩漬けし、発酵・熟成した魚醤油ともよばれる郷土調味料。秋田のしょっつる、能登のいしるなどが有名。
A local seasoning also called fish soy sauce made by salting, fermenting, and aging fish. In Japan, Akita prefecture's Shottsuru, or Noto Peninsula's Irushi are well-known.

和の材 | Japanese Ingredients

092 みりん
Mirin

日本特有の調味料で、焼き物、煮物などに照りとツヤを出すために使います。餅米、米麹焼酎で醸造され、素材の臭みをとり、甘みを加え、旨みを引き出すもの。煮崩れ防止効果も。熱を加えない和えものやタレに使う時に、ひと手間を惜しまずやってみてほしいのは、一度みりんを沸騰するまで加熱して煮切ること。アルコール臭が飛び、さらに甘みと香りが強くなり、風味も増します。ついでに、煮切るという言葉はみりんと日本酒のみに使う言葉のようです。

Sweat Sake: This seasoning unique to Japan is used to glaze or add a bright touch to grilled and simmered dishes. Brewed from glutinous rice, rice koji, and shochu, it removes the ingredients' smell, adds sweetness, and brings out the umami. It also prevents them from becoming mushy. Try to bring it to boil and reduce it all the way when using for uncooked aemono or sauces. This removes the alcoholic smell and increases the sweetness and aroma. The word 'nikiru' (to boil down) is apparently used only with mirin and sake.

093 料理酒
Ryori-shu

調味料としての酒は、そのまま飲んでも美味しいものを使いましょう。酒は食材の保存力を高めたり、味を引き立て、ふくよかな旨みを引き出してくれます。みりんと同様に煮切って使うこともあり、酒と梅干しを煮切って作るのを煎り酒といいます。醤油の代用品として江戸時代から使われていた、手作りの万能調味料。今では、料亭や寿司屋などでだしなども加えた贅沢な調味料として、相性のよい白身魚のたれとして使われています。最近は市販もあり、減塩とまろやかな風味が人気になっています。

Japanese Cooking Sake: Use sake that tastes good on its own since it's an essential condiment for Japanese food. It preserves ingredients longer, enhances the flavor, and brings out the rich umami. Irizake is made by putting sour plum in sake and boiling down. It was a homemade seasoning used in the Edo period as a substitute for soy sauce. Nowadays ryotei or sushi restaurants may use it as sauce for white fish with dashi added to enrich the flavors. The ones with reduced salt and mild flavors are popular on the market.

| 和の材 | Japanese Ingredients |

094 胡麻油
Goma-abura

胡麻の実から搾油した油で、歴史は古く仏教の伝来とともに日本に入り、江戸時代に広がったそうです。ビタミンEやリノール酸が多く含まれているので、美容と健康にもよいといわれています。胡麻の焙煎の度合いで色が変わり、深く煎った濃口はラーメン、餃子などの中華や香り付けに、浅く煎った淡口は香りがやわらかく、天ぷらなどの揚げもの、炒めもの、ドレッシングなどに向いています。

Sesame Oil: This oil pressed from sesame seeds is said to have entered Japan along with the introduction of Buddhism, spreading during the Edo period. With a great aroma, it's used for aemono (chopped fish or vegetables dressed in sauce) and fried and grilled food. It's resistant to oxidation and rich in linoleic acid, making it a popular choice for its health benefits. The color changes depending on the degree of sesame roasting; the dark-roasted koikuchi is suitable for ramen, gyoza dumplings, or flavoring for Chinese cuisine, while the light-roasted awakuchi has a milder aroma and is best for fried food like tempura, stir-fries, and dressings.

095 ソース
Sosu

ソースは日本の開国時に、イギリスからウスターソースが入ってきたのが始まりで、国産ソースの製造は明治後期からです。ソースはとろみ具合で種類がわかれていて、主原料の野菜や果実、香辛料の配合でその違いを出しています。関西ではウスターソース、関東では中濃ソースを常備する家庭が多いといわれています。私はカレーやドミグラスソースを作る時に、ウスターソースを隠し味に使います。

Sauce: Essential to dishes like hambagu, yakisoba, or okonomiyaki, the first type of sauce was introduced from the UK as Worcester sauce when Japan opened up. It became generally popular only in the late Meiji period once domestic sauce began to be produced. Since it originated in the Kansai region, apparently sauce there refers to Worcester sauce. Many types of sauces exist depending on the consistency, which changes based on the ratio of the main ingredients such as vegetables, fruits, and spices.

ウスターソース
Usuta Sosu
さらりとした口あたりでほどよい辛さが特長。関西では多用される。
Known for its light taste and perfect amount of spiciness, it's widely used in the Kansai region.

とんかつソース
Tonkatsu Sosu
果実を多く使用しているので、甘くとろりとしたソフトな味わい。
It's thick and mild taste comes from all the fruit that is used.

中濃ソース
Chuno Sosu
ウスターととんかつの真ん中で、ほどよい甘みとびりっとした風味。
A mix between Worcester and tonkatsu sauce with a perfectly sweet and refreshing flavor.

お好みソース
Okonomi Sosu
他のソースに比べ香辛料が多く、塩分がひかえめ。お好み焼きには欠かせない。
Essential for okonomiyaki, it's rich in spices compared to other sauces and contains less salt.

和の材 | Japanese Ingredients

096 味噌
Miso

味噌は醤油と並ぶ、日本の食文化に欠かせない発酵調味料の代表格ですが、歴史は醤油より古いといわれています。古代中国の醤が起源で、工夫が重ねられ、室町時代には貴重な大豆からのタンパク源として、味噌汁を飲むようになったそうです。ゆでた大豆をつぶして、麹と塩を混ぜ、発酵・熟成して作るシンプルな製造方法。昔は各家庭で作られてきたので「手前味噌」の言葉も生まれたほど。最近はまた自家製の味噌作りがブームになっています。味噌は地方色が強く、材料・風味・色にそれぞれ特色があります。代表的なものをあげてみました。

Fermented Soybean Paste: Although miso, along with soy sauce, is a fermented condiment symbolic of Japanese food culture, it's even older than soy sauce. Originating in ancient Chinese hishio, by the Muromachi period through many trials and errors it became consumed as a source of soybean protein in the form of miso soup. The production method is simple, consisting of crushing steamed soybeans and mixing it with koji and salt to ferment and age. In the past, each family produced their own miso, which created the word "temae-miso." Homemade miso is recently regaining its popularity.

豆味噌
Mame Miso

豆麹を使い、熟成期間が長いため濃い赤茶色が特徴。代表的なものは愛知の八丁味噌。

Red Miso: Soybean koji based miso with a reddish brown color due to the long fermentation period. The most well-known type is Aichi's Hatcho miso.

米味噌
Kome Miso

米麹を使った多くの地域で作られている、仙台味噌などの通称田舎味噌。

Brown Miso: This miso uses soybean, rice koji, and salt and is produced in various areas. It's also known as inaka miso (countryside miso).

白味噌
Shiro Miso

大豆より米麹の割合が多く甘口。代表的なもので関西の西京味噌、和菓子にも使われる。

White Miso: Tastes sweet with a higher proportion of koji than soybean. Originating in the Kansai region, it's also called Saikyo miso and used in Japanese sweets.

麦味噌
Mugi Miso

麦麹を使った麦味噌は、九州や四国などが発祥。麹の香りと甘みが強い。

Barley Miso: Miso originating in the Kyushu and Shikoku regions, that uses barley, malt and has a unique scent and flavor.

| 和の材 | Japanese Ingredients

097 だし
Dashi

世界の料理界が注目する日本のだし。「旨み」という日本語もそのまま使われています。この旨みが和食の原点、基本の味です。だしをとる素材には、昆布、鰹節、いりこ、しいたけなどがあります。水に浸した後に加熱してだしをとるという、世界の中でも一番簡単にとれるだしといえるかもしれません。汁物、煮物、うどん・そばのつゆなど、あらゆる料理に多用されます。一般的な一番だしの昆布と鰹節のだしには、昆布のグルタミン酸、鰹節のイノシン酸が多く含まれていて、この2つが合わさり強力な相乗効果でさらに旨みが倍増するといわれています。

Dashi Stock: Japanese dashi is attracting the global culinary industry's attention. Even the word "umami," or the unique flavor that forms the basis of Japanese food, is directly used in English. Ingredients such as kelp, bonito, dried sardines, or shiitake mushrooms are simply soaked in water then brought to a boil, making dashi one of the easiest stocks to prepare. It's widely used for soup, simmered dishes, and dipping sauce for udon or soba. Since kelp is rich in glutamic acid and bonito contains a large amount of inosinic acid, the combination of the two creates a synergistic effect that strengthens this umami flavor.

一番だしのとりかた
How to Make Dashi Stock

［味噌汁2人分］
昆布……5g
鰹節……10g
水……500cc

Serves two cups of Miso Soup:
5 grams kelp
10 grams bonito flakes
500 ml water

❶ 昆布の表面の汚れを乾いた布でふき、鍋の水に最低30分はつけておく（旨みを抽出しやすくする）。
Clean the surface of the kelp with a dry cloth and soak it in the water in the pot for at least 30 minutes. This enhances the umami extraction.

❷ 鍋を火にかけて、昆布の表面に気泡がでてきたら中火にし、沸騰直前に昆布を取り出す。
Heat the water and once bubbles emerge on the kelp surface, bring to medium heat. Remove the kelp right before it comes to a full boil.

❸ そのまま火にかけ、再び沸騰したら鰹節を鍋に入れる。
Continue to heat the water and when it comes to a boil again, add the bonito flakes.

❹ 火をそのままにし、沸騰したら火を止めて、鰹節が下に沈むまで2分ほど待つ。
Let the water come to a boil and remove the pan from heat. Let the bonito steep in the stock for about 2 minutes.

❺ ざるにキッチンペーパーをしき、鍋のだしを漉す。臭みがでるので鰹節を押したりしない。
Cover the strainer with a paper towel and strain the dashi. To avoid extracting the smell, do not squeeze the bonito.

125

| Japanese Ingredients

098 乾物
Kambutsu

日本には豊富な種類の乾物があり、昔から日々の食事に登場する伝統食品です。海苔、昆布などの海草類、海老、鰹などの魚介類、うどん、そばなどの穀類、キノコ、豆などの野菜類など。天日にさらすことにより栄養分が凝縮され、水分が除かれ、細菌を防ぎ、長期保存を可能にする、古来からの人間の知恵が凝縮されています。見た目は地味ですが、栄養価も高く、幅広い料理に活用できます。私は防災用の非常食として完備しています。例えば、高野豆腐は砕いてお湯を注げば重湯のような栄養価のある一食になります。

Dried Food: A rich assortment of kanbutsu exists in Japan, serving as essential food items for daily meals. Examples include seaweed like nori and kelp, seafood like shrimp and bonito, grains like udon or soba, and vegetables like mushrooms and beans. It's ancient human wisdom condensed into a technique; exposure to the sun compresses the nutrients, removes the moisture, kills bacteria, and allows for long term preservation. Although they may look bland, they are packed with nutrients and used in a variety of dishes.

ひじき Hijiki
海岸近くの岩場で穫れる海藻。茎は長ひじき、芽の部分は芽ひじきになる。
Seaweed harvested in the rocky area near the coast, its stem becomes long hijiki, and its sprout becomes mehjiki.

高野豆腐 Koya-dofu
豆腐を凍結、低温熟成し乾燥させたもの。水に戻すと倍の大きさになる。
Made by freezing tofu and aging it at low temperature before drying, it becomes twice its size when soaked in water.

切り干し大根 Kiriboshi-daikon
大根を千切りにして乾燥させた保存食。戻す時間は短く、アクも出ない。
A preservative food consisting of dried radish strips, it quickly rehydrates and does not produce scum.

干し海老 Hoshi-ebi
桜えびなど小エビを素干ししたもの。カルシウム分が非常に高い。だしもよくとれる。
Sakura shrimps or shrimps dried in the shade, it's very high in calcium.

ひじき煮
Hijiki-ni
お惣菜の定番の一品。作りたてより、1日置くと味が しみ込んで美味しくなります。
Simmered Hijiki Seaweed: A staple of side dishes, it's paired up with carrots and fried tofu, and beans to add color.

高野豆腐の煮物
Koya-Dofu no Nimono
高野山から広まった精進料理。甘めの味付けにした ほうが美味しく、残ったら細かく切って混ぜ寿司に。
Simmered Koya-Dofu: Shojin-ryori, or Japanese Buddhist cuisine, spread from Mount Koya. The tip is to allow the tofu to soak up plenty of the dashi and to sweeten it when seasoning.

切り干し大根の煮物
Kiriboshi-Daikon no Nimono
冷ますと醤油味が濃く感じるので、少し甘めに仕上 げます。
Simmered Kiriboshi-Daikon: Any family's go-to side dish, it goes well with rice. Leave the crispy texture and sweeten it a bit for a final touch.

| Japanese Ingredients

099 海藻
Kaiso

海に囲まれている日本列島は、海藻の宝庫です。昆布、あおさ、寒天、海苔など乾物になっているものも多いですが、もずく、わかめ、めこんぶなど生食で食べる海藻も多彩です。食物繊維、マグネシウム、カルシウム、亜鉛、鉄などミネラルが豊富で、水溶性食物繊維は老廃物を追い出す効果があり、海のスーパーフードといわれています。

Seaweed: The Japanese archipelago, surrounded by the ocean, is a seaweed treasure trove. Many such as kelp, aosa (sea lettuce), kanten (Japanese agar), and nori are dry food, but there is also a variety of fresh seaweed such as mozuku, wakame, and mekonbu. Rich in minerals, fiber, magnesium, calcium, zinc, and iron, with water soluble fiber effective in processing bodily waste, it's the ocean's superfood.

海藻サラダ Kaiso Salada
わかめ、赤つのまた、白きくらげ、寒天など多種類の海藻を味わえるサラダです。海藻のたんぱくな味には、しそや梅風味のドレッシングがよく合います。他に、そばサラダの具材やインスタントラーメンのトッピングにすると栄養価アップにも。

Seaweed Salad: This is a salad perfect for enjoying various types of seaweed such as wakame, aka-tsunomata (red algae), shiro-kikurage (snow fungus), and kanten (Japanese agar). It goes well with shiso or plum flavored dressing.

わかめの酢のもの
Wakame no Sunomono

最初に酢のものを食べると唾液が出て、飲み込みやすくなるといいます。わかめの水気をしっかりと切ることで、酢のなじみがよくなります。

This is a classic wakame recipe that never gets boring. By draining the ingredients thoroughly, they blend well with the vinegar.

もずく酢
Mozuku-su

もずくと三杯酢の簡単レシピ。おろした生姜をしぼって三杯酢に入れ、さらに上にのせると風味が増します。スープにするのもおすすめ。

An easy dish made of mozuku and sanbaizu (a mixture of vinegar, soy sauce, and sugar), it becomes even more flavorful by adding grated ginger in the sanbaizu and as topping.

和の材　　Japanese Ingredients

100 香辛料
Koshinryo

スパイスとハーブは明確な線引きで分類することはできませんが、ここでは、種や根などのスパイスを香辛料として、葉ものなどはハーブとしてご紹介することにします。日本は昔から、山の幸、海の幸に恵まれ、新鮮な食材を料理に取り入れてきました。奈良時代の古事記などに生姜、山椒、からし、わさびなどが、すでに記されているほど。日本の香辛料は、おもに食材を引き立てる薬味、腐敗防止や臭み抜きとして、辛味、香り、色付けなどに使います。西洋のスパイスと違い、七味などを除いて、単体で使うのが特徴だといえます。

Japanese Spices: Although spices and herbs cannot be differentiated clearly, here are some spices derived from seeds and roots and herbs as leafy greens. Historically, Japan

生姜　Shoga
刻んだり、すりおろして使う。食材の臭みを消す効果がある。新生姜の甘酢漬は初夏に1年分まとめて作りおく。
Ginger: The sweet and sour pickled ginger maintains its permanent spot as the perfect sushi garnish. Chopped or grated, it's a versatile condiment.

わさび　Wasabi
日本特産で水のきれいな渓流に自生する。おろすと茎側は香りよく辛味が少ない。先端側は香りが弱いが辛みは強い。
A Japanese specialty, it naturally grows in mountain streams. The sharp sting essential for sushi and sashimi is popular all around the world.

和がらし　Wagarashi
マスタードと比べるとにおいも辛みも強く、苦みもある風味豊かな和がらし。からし菜の種を乾燥させ粉砕している。
Japanese Mustard: Spicy, slightly bitter, and containing a strong smell, jigarashi (local mustard) is packed with flavors. It's made by crushing seeds.

実山椒　Mizansho
山椒の成熟した実を実山椒とよび、佃煮や粉山椒として使われる。ピリッとした辛味とすがすがしい風味が特長。
Green Japanese Peppercorn: Mizansho refers to the matured fruit of the sansho pepper. Used for tsukudani (food simmered in soy sauce) or in powder form, it has a unique flavor.

has enjoyed the rich fruits of the sea and the mountain, and the cuisine has incorporated fresh ingredients. This is evident in the fact that *Records of Ancient Matters* written in the Nara period already included descriptions of ginger, Japanese pepper, mustard, and wasabi. Japanese condiments are used to enhance the flavor, prevent rotting, and remove the odor of the ingredients, adding spiciness, aroma, and color. Unlike Western spices, with the exception of shichimi (seven spice mixture), the characteristic of Japanese condiments is that they are used on their own.

青唐辛子 Aotogarashi
赤くなる前に収穫した唐辛子。加熱すると辛さが和らぎ、ほんのりと甘くなる。ゆず胡椒作りに欠かせない。
Green Chili: Aotogarashi refers to chili that is harvested before turning red. When cooked, it becomes less spicy and slightly sweet.

柚子 Yuzu
日本の柑橘類の代表格。香味付けに皮を削って使う。また、完熟したものは、風呂に入れて柚子湯にも。
One of the most common citrus fruits in Japan, it's used by scraping the skin for flavoring. Put matured yuzu in the tub to enjoy a yuzu bath.

胡麻 Goma
古来から世界中で食されている栄養価の高い胡麻。かける、和えるはもちろん、フライの衣としても使える。
Sesame: Consumed all over the world since ancient times, it contains all nutrients besides Vitamin C.

くちなし Kuchinashi
きんとんの色付けや漢方に幅広く使われる食物。乾燥した実のまま、または粉にして使う。
Gardenia: This is used as garnish for candied chestnuts and incorporated widely in traditional Chinese medicine. The fruit is dried or powdered.

| 和の材 | Japanese Ingredients |

101 和のハーブ
Wa no Habu

ハーブというと、西洋料理に使うタイムやローズマリーなどをすぐに思い浮かべると思いますが、日本にも多くの伝統的なハーブがあります。日本の風土で育ち、昔から日本人の食生活に活用され、健康促進に役立つ旬の野草、香草、薬草が日本のハーブです。身近なものでは、しそや山椒は、香り付けや殺菌力を活かして刺身など生ものに利用しています。薬効の強いドクダミ、柿、びわの葉などは昔から薬草の健康茶として親しまれてきました。また、七草粥に入れる七草も、古来からの日本の野草です。ここでは、薬味として一般的なもの、旬の料理には欠かせないものをあげてみました。

Japanese Herbs: When considering herbs, you may associate ones used in Western cuisine such as thyme or rosemary, but

しそ Shiso
香りに食欲増進効果がある。防腐効果もあり、料理の添え物、薬味などに使うほか、お弁当に入れて抗菌効果を活用。
The shiso aroma boosts your appetite; this herb is also used as a preservative garnish.

三つ葉 Mitsuba
汁物に浮かべて香り付けとして使う。ミネラル、ビタミン類が豊富。根三つ葉は香りが強いので卵とじがおすすめ。
Used as topping on soups for its aroma, it's rich in minerals and vitamins.

せり Seri
各地の山野に自生する。春の七草の一つで、万病を防ぐといわれる。きりたんぽ鍋には欠かせない。
This herb grows naturally in various mountains and fields. One of the seven spring herbs in the Festival of Seven Herbs, it's believed to cure all kinds of illnesses and is used in one-pot meals.

山椒 Sansho
若芽は木の芽と呼ばれ、吸い物や和えものに使う。辛みは胃腸に効くといわれる。使う前に一度たたくと香りが増す。
Young buds are called kinome, and are used in suimono (clear soups) and aemono (vegetables dressed in sauce). The spiciness is said to promote digestive health.

Japanese herbs consist of spice plants essential to Japanese cooking. They are local and seasonal edible plants, herbs, and medicinal herbs that have been traditionally used in Japanese food, packed with health-promoting benefits. The scent and sterilizing effect is used for raw foods like sashimi, while medicinal ones like dokudami, persimmon, or loquat leaf have long been popular in making healthy teas and medicinal herbs. Here are some general condiments and essentials for seasonal cooking.

春菊 Shungiku
独特な香りに消化促進効果がある。カロテンの含有量はほうれん草より多い。ジェノベーゼソースで作り置くと便利。
Edible Chrysanthemum: The unique scent promotes digestion. It contains more beta-carotene than spinach.

あさつき Asatsuki
ネギ類の中で一番細く、独特な香りと辛みがある。薬味に使う。まとめて小口切りにし冷凍しておくと便利。
Chives: The thinnest among the onion family, it has a distinct scent and bitterness. It's used as a condiment.

みょうが Myoga
各地に自生している香味植物。香り成分に食欲増進効果があり、夏バテに効く。甘酢漬けにするときれいな色になる。
Japanese Ginger: A flavoring plant that grows locally throughout Japan, the aroma increases one's appetite and prevents summer heat fatigue.

えごま Egoma
シソ科の葉物で、風味は独特。野菜としてよりも油をとるのに多く使われる。えごまオイルは火を通さずに使う。
Perilla: Although it's a leafy green of the Labiatae family, it has a unique flavor. It's used more for extracting the oil rather than cooking it as a vegetable.

和の道具
Japanese Tools

まな板と包丁
Cutting Board & Knife

和食の料理人のことを板前、または包丁人といいます。これはまな板と包丁が和食作りの基本にはとても重要なものである、ということを表わしているからでしょう。家庭ではプラスチック製が主流になりつつあるまな板ですが、木製は刃当たりの良さが違います。木の弾力性で、手にも、包丁にも優しく、刃こぼれもしにくいのです。まな板に使われる木は主に、桐、檜、銀杏などがあります。また、包丁も家庭ではステンレス製が多く使われますが、鋼(はがね)を使った包丁は硬さ、切れ味が抜群です。日本の包丁は世界に誇れる職人技で、世界から訪れる多くの人が買い求めていくほどです。定期的に砥石を使い包丁を研ぐことも大事です。今は便利なシャープナーもあるので、手間をおしまないようにしましょう。切れない包丁では美味しい料理は作れません。いい道具も手入れあってこそです。

Japanese chefs are called itamae or hochonin in Japanese, which are words derived from mana-ita (cutting board) and hocho (knife). The cutting board and the knife together are the most essential elements in Japanese cooking. Although plastic cutting boards are becoming more frequently used in homes, wooden cutting boards produce the finest cuts. The elasticity of the wood works gently with your hands and the knife, making it less likely to chip the knife. The main woods used for cutting boards include paulownia, cypress, and ginkgo among others. At home stainless steel knives are frequently used, but carbon steel knives excel in their hardness and sharpness. Japanese knives are known worldwide for their superior craftsmanship. Regularly sharpening your knife with a whetstone is crucial, since no good meal will be served with a dull knife. Having good tools also means maintaining them well.

包丁の種類　Various Types of Knives

Ⓐ 柳刃包丁　Yanagiba-bocho
刺身包丁の代表的なもので、切れ味の鋭さが特長。
One of the most common sashimi knives, it's known for its extra sharpness.

Ⓑ 出刃包丁　Deba-bocho
魚を下ろすための刃が厚い包丁。骨も簡単に切れる重さ。
A thick-bladed knife used to gut and fillet fish, it's sturdy enough to easily slice fish bones.

Ⓒ 菜切り包丁　Nakkiri-bocho
先端がない四角い刃の野菜などを切る包丁。両刃で薄い。
Used for cutting vegetables, this knife's back edge tip is squared while the cutting edge is thin and angled from both sides, which is called ryoba.

Ⓓ 牛刀　Gyuto
世界中で広く使われている西洋包丁。肉を切るのに便利。
A Western knife widely used all over the world, it's useful for cutting meat.

Ⓔ 三徳包丁　Santoku-bocho
肉、魚、野菜の三つを扱うという意味の万能包丁。
An all-purpose knife, the name santoku refers to handling the three types of food-meat, fish, and vegetables.

| 和の道具 | Japanese Tools |

鍋類
Pots

文化鍋　Bunka-nabe
炊飯ジャーが広まるまでは、どの家庭でも大活躍していたアルミニウム炊飯用鍋。吹きこぼれ防止で、フタが鍋の縁より2～3cm低いのが特徴です。
This is an aluminum rice cooking pot that used to be found in every Japanese household until rice cookers became more common. It's characterized by a lid that settles 2 to 3 centimeters below the rim of the pot, which prevents the liquid from boiling over.

土鍋　Donabe
じっくりとしっかりと熱が伝わる陶磁器の土鍋は、鍋料理はもとより、ごはんも美味しく炊くことができます。
The ceramic donabe pot distributes and holds heat efficiently, which makes it perfect not only for one-pot dishes but also for cooking delicious rice.

行平（雪平）Yukihira-nabe
木製の柄がついた、汁の注ぎ口がついたものが一般的。アルミ製が多く、熱の伝導率が高く調理も素早くできます。昔からある万能鍋。
The most common type has a wooden handle and a spout for soups and sauces. Many are made from aluminum. This traditional, all-purpose pot has high conductivity and allows for quick cooking.

やかん Yakan

昔ながらのレトロなアルミのやかん。世界中で使われているケトルは、ステンレスやホーローが主流ですが、アルミはすぐにお湯が沸くのがいいところです。

Japanese yakan kettles are traditionally made from aluminum, producing a retro feel. Although stainless steel or enamel ones are more common for this universal tool, aluminum ones are useful since the water boils quickly.

急須 Kyusu

緑茶などを入れる急須は陶磁器などの瀬戸物が主流ですが、こんなステンレス製タイプの急須も。昔のアルミ製の復刻版も風情があっていいものです。

This teapot used for brewing green tea and other teas and is most commonly made of ceramic ware such as setomono. This type of stainless steel teapot is a reproduction of the old aluminum type.

鉄瓶 Tetsubin

鋳物である鉄瓶の歴史は江戸時代から。鉄瓶で沸かすお湯は鉄分を含み、体に吸収されやすく、お茶なども美味しくいれられます。

The cast-iron tetsubin traces its beginning to the Edo period. Water boiled with it contains iron that is easily absorbed in the body and makes delicious tea.

竹の道具
Bamboo Wood Tools

つみれ器 Tsumire-ki

鍋用のつみれ製造器。竹筒のところに鶏肉などのつみれを入れ、ヘラで団子状にして鍋に入れます。目の前で調理する楽しみも増えます。

A tsumire maker for hot pots, it's used by putting minced chicken or other ingredients into the bamboo cylinder, rolling it into a ball shape then adding it to the hot pot. It's fun to watch it being prepared at the dinner table.

おろし刷毛 Oroshi-hake

わさび、柚子、生姜などをおろし器からかき寄せる刷毛。好きな分量をきれいにおろし金からとれるので、1つあると便利です。

This brush is used to collect grated ingredients like wasabi, yuzu, and ginger from the oroshigane grater. It's quite satisfying to cleanly brush off your preferred amount from the grater.

菜箸 Sai-bashi

調理箸の野菜用なので菜箸と呼ばれています。他に魚用として真魚箸（まなばし）があり、味が移るのを防ぐために使い分けをします。竹製は丈夫で軽いのが特長です。

These are useful cooking chopsticks essential in the kitchen for stir-frying, frying, grilling, dressing, and garnishing. Bamboo ones are sturdy and light.

巻きす Makisu

巻き寿司を作る時には欠かせない巻きす。海苔のサイズに合わせてありますが、卵焼きの型を整形する時などにも使えます。

An essential tool for making rolled makizushi, it's seaweed-sized but also used to shape tamagoyaki eggs.

ざる Zaru

伝統工芸の網目の美しい竹ざる。水切りや野菜入れ、麺類、天ぷらなどの皿として使うなど、様々に活用できます。

These traditional Japanese strainers are beautifully woven and versatile, used as a strainer, vegetable holder, or serving plate for soba, udon, or tempura.

茶こし Cha-koshi

昔ながらの竹製の茶こしは風情があり、お茶をいれるのが楽しくなります。茶こしの他に、鍋料理でも食材の湯煎に使えます。

The classic bamboo tea strainer provides an elegant feel to the act of brewing tea. Besides straining tea, it can also be used for boiling ingredients when making hot pot.

蒸籠 Seiro

蒸籠は中華蒸籠と和蒸籠があります。竹で編んだフタと中敷が固定式なのが中華蒸籠で、和蒸籠は厚い木のフタと取り外し可能な中敷が特徴です。

These steamers can be divided into the two types of Chinese seiro and Japanese seiro. Chinese seiro has a bamboo-woven lid and a fixed inner base, serving as an all-purpose steamer for fish, vegetables, dim sum, and more.

木の道具
Wooden Tools

しゃもじ Shamoji
使う前に水で濡らすのが基本で、ごはん粒がつきにくくなります。ほのかに木の香りもしてプラスチックよりがぜん風情があります。
Always dip it in water before using to keep the rice from sticking. Wooden ones give off a subtle aroma and are much more tasteful than plastic ones.

おひつ Ohitsu
炊きたてのごはんをおひつに移して保存すると、木が余分な水分を吸ってくれ、ごはんの甘みを保ち、理想的なごはんの食感になります。
Transfer freshly cooked rice into an ohitsu to preserve it well. The wood absorbs the extra moisture and maintains the sweetness of the rice, creating an ideal texture.

飯台 Handai
さわらを使った桶は、水に強く、殺菌性があります。飯台を使って寿司飯を作ると、おひつと同じで、余分な水分を木が吸ってくれ、美味しい寿司飯ができます。
Sawara cypress tubs are resistant to water and bacteria. When making sushi rice with a handai, allowing the wood to absorb the extra moisture of the rice results in delicious sushi rice.

押し寿司器　Oshizushi-ki

鯖などを押し寿司にするのは関西が発祥で、こういった木箱に詰めて形を作ります。彩りよく海老や鮭などを使って作るときれいです。

Fish such as mackerel are stuffed into wooden boxes to make pressed sushi, which originated in the Kansai region. Add shrimp or salmon to make the colors pop.

落とし蓋　Otoshi-buta

鍋よりひと回り小さい落とし蓋を使い、鍋の材料が煮崩れしないように押さえたり、味をしみ込ませたりする時に使います。

A lid that is smaller in diameter than the pot, it's useful for gently keeping the materials in their original shape and allowing the flavor to be absorbed.

鮫皮おろし　Samegawa-oroshi

鮫の皮を木製の台に貼付けたわさび専用のおろし器。クリーミーで香りがよく、まろやかなわさびに仕上がります。

A wasabi grater made of sharkskin fixed onto a wooden board, it produces creamy, fragrant, and smooth wasabi.

黒文字楊枝　Kuromoji-yoji

楊枝も様々ありますが、香り高い黒文字の木を使った楊枝は、和菓子を頂く時に使います。しなやかで弾力性がありささくれがないのが特長。

Although there are various kinds of yoji toothpicks, the kuromoji ones made from fragrant wood are used when eating Japanese sweets. It's supple, elastic, and splinter-free.

和の道具 | Japanese Tools

金物・瀬戸物道具
Hardware and Pottery Goods

おろし金　Oroshigane
大根おろし、生姜、にんにくなどの
薬味おろしに使うおろし金。ステン
レスの刀の切れ味は抜群です。
A sharp grater used to grate
condiments like daikon radish,
ginger, and garlic.

骨抜き　Honenuki
魚の下処理に使う骨抜き。しなやかなバネ
感で大きな骨も小さな骨も力を入れずに軽
く抜けるのがスゴいです。
A fish de-boner used for preparing fish.
It's quite impressive how the pliable spring
allows easy removal of both large and
small bones without force.

豆腐すくい　Tofu-sukui
湯豆腐の鍋から豆腐をすくう専用の
金網。繊細な平らな網目で豆腐を滑
らせず、崩さずすくうことができます。
A wired tool to scoop tofu from a
yudofu, or tofu hot pot, the delicate
and flat mesh scoops it up without
losing its shape.

胡麻炒り器　Gomairi-ki
フライパンで胡麻を炒るとはねて飛び散って大変。これは
網目のフタがついた胡麻飛び防止をする専用の道具です。
It's quite tedious when the sesame seeds splash
everywhere upon roasting them in a pan. This tool has
a meshed lid that prevents the sesame from spilling out.

卵焼き器　Tamagoyaki-ki
プロも使う銅製の卵焼き器は、熱
伝導がいいのでふんわりとした卵
焼きが作れます。関東は正方形、
関西は長方形と形が違います。
Copper tamagoyaki pans are even
used by professionals since its
high heat conductivity produces
fluffy eggs. They are square-
shaped in the Kanto region while
rectangle-shaped in the Kansai
region. The most common pans
are the non-stick coated ones that
are easy to use.

すり鉢・すりこぎ Suri-bachi & Suri-kogi

胡麻だれ、白和え、酢みそ、和えものに欠かせない。山芋をすってだしを入れたとろろ芋は、このまま食卓に出してもOKです。

This mortar is essential for Japanese cooking, whether it's for grinding fragrant sesame to dress it with vegetables, tofu for a shira-ae (mashed tofu salad), or Japanese mountain yam for tororo. It can also be used as a bowl for serving food.

魚焼き器 Sakanayaki-ki

コンロにのせて魚を焼く昔からの魚焼き器。野菜や肉、おにぎりを焼いたりと、いろいろ活用できます。

A traditional tool now used to broil fish in the built-in broiler of a stove, it can be used for various types of food such as vegetables, meat, or grilled rice balls.

銀杏むき Ginnan-muki

銀杏の皮むき専用の道具。先端のくぼみに銀杏を入れて、やさしく割り中身を取り出します。

A peeler for gingko nuts, it's used by putting the gingko in the hole at the tip and gently cracking it to take out the nutmeats.

ヘラ Hera

お好み焼きの本場関西ではコテ、広島はテコ、関東はヘラと呼びます。お好み焼きに不可欠な道具です。

This is called a kote in the Kansai region (home to okonomiyaki), a teko in Hiroshima, and a hera in the Kanto region. It's an indispensable tool for flipping okonomiyaki.

おたま Otama

正式にはお玉杓子といい、オタマジャクシに似ているところから名付けられたレードル。アルミ製はレトロ感満載。

A type of ladle that is officially called an otamajakushi since it resembles a tadpole.

網じゃくし Amijakushi

天ぷらの天かすをすくう網じゃくし、アクをすくうアク取りとは厳密には分けられていますが、兼用もあります。

Although amijakushi, which is used to scoop the crispy bits of tempura batter, and akutori, which is used to scoop the scum, are strictly divided, they may be used for both occasions.

一汁三菜の配膳

Setting up the Table for Ichiju-Sansai
with Japanese Tableware

ここでは和食の基本である一汁三菜の正しい配膳、器のあつかい方をおさらいしておきましょう。和食の作法を一度覚えておくと安心です。食べる順番は、汁碗からが基本。また、汁碗、飯茶碗、副々菜の器は持ち上げ、主菜、副菜は持ち上げずに食べます。

Ⓐ 飯茶碗は汁碗の左側におく。手に持って食べる。
Ⓑ 汁碗は飯茶碗の右側。箸を使って手に持って飲む。
Ⓒ 主菜は右上に。平らな大ぶりな皿に盛る。
Ⓓ 副菜は左上に。大ぶりの鉢に盛る。
Ⓔ 副々菜は中央に置く。小ぶりな軽い小鉢に盛る。

Let's review the correct table setting and tableware handling for ichiju-sansai, or one soup and three dishes (with rice), which forms the basis of Japanese cuisine. Once you learn Japanese table manners, it will take you a long way. Start your meal first with the soup bowl. When eating, lift up the soup bowl, rice bowl, and plates of the sub-side dishes, but do not lift up the plates of the main dish or side dish.

Ⓐ Place the rice bowl to the left of the soup bowl. Hold the rice bowl in your hand when eating it.
Ⓑ Place the soup bowl to the right of the rice bowl. Hold the soup bowl in your hand and use your chopsticks when drinking it.
Ⓒ Place the main dish to the upper right side. Serve it on a flat, large plate.
Ⓓ Place the side dish to the upper left side. Serve it in a large bowl.
Ⓔ Place the sub-side dish in the middle. Serve it in a small, light bowl.

正しい箸のあつかい方
Back to the Basics: How to Use Chopsticks

ものごころついてから、毎日箸を使っている日本人ですが、箸を上手に使えていないと思っている人が意外と多いとか。世界中で約3割の人が箸でごはんを食べていますが、日本は食事の最初から最後まで箸だけで食べる世界で唯一の国だといわれています。もう一度、箸を正しく使うマナーをおさらいしてみましょう。

Although Japanese people start using chopsticks as soon as they can walk and talk, a surprising number of people apparently don't use them well. About 30% of the world's population uses chopsticks, but Japan's the only country where people eat the entire meal just using chopsticks. Let's review how to correctly use chopsticks.

❶ 箸おきに置かれている箸を右手で取る。
Take the chopsticks from the chopstick rest with your right hand.

❷ 左手の親指、人差し指、中指で箸を下からささえて持つ。
Place your left hand beneath the chopsticks to support them with your left thumb, index finger, and middle finger.

❸ 右手を箸の下に回して持つ。左手はそえたまま。
Place your right hand beneath the chopsticks. Keep your left hand in the same position.

❹ 親指、人差し指で上の箸、中指、薬指で下の箸をささえる。下の箸は動かさず、上だけ動かす。
Use your thumb and index finger to support the upper chopstick, and your middle finger and ring finger to support the lower one. Only move the upper chopstick to adjust the width in between.

やってはいけない箸の使い方　Bad Chopstick Manners

箸の使い方の禁じ手、やってはいけない箸の使い方を「嫌い箸」といいます。そのマナーに反する使い方は70手以上数えられるそうです。ここでは、ついやってしまいがちなものをあげてみました。

Kirai-bashi (literally "hate chopsticks") refers to the taboos of using chopsticks. Over 70 terms are said to exist for bad chopstick manners. Here are some especially common ones.

寄せ箸　Yose-bashi
箸を使って器を動かす。
Using the chopsticks to move plates on the table.

渡し箸　Watashi-bashi
食事途中に器の上におく。
Placing the chopsticks on plates and bowls when taking a break or finishing the meal.

刺し箸　Sashi-bashi
食べ物に箸を刺す。
Sticking the chopsticks into the food.

立て箸　Tate-bashi
箸をごはんに突き立てる。
Sticking the chopsticks vertically in rice.

二人箸　Futari-bashi
一緒に同じものをはさむ。
To grab the same thing simultaneously as someone else, or to pass them food.

回し箸　Mawashi-bashi
汁などをぐるぐるかき回す。
Stirring soup items like miso soup with the chopsticks.

割り箸の使い方　Dos and Don'ts of Disposable Chopsticks

割り箸は、箸先を左にして横に持ち、上下に割る。縦に持って、左右に割ったりこすり合わせたりしない。

Do hold the chopsticks sideways with the tips on the left side, then split them vertically.
Don't hold the chopsticks vertically and split them right and left.
Don't rub the chopsticks together.

149

和の器
Japanese Pottery

和の器は、洋食器に比べると大きさや形も様々で、用途別の種類の多さも驚くほどあります。素材も陶器や磁器、木器から漆器まで、伝統工芸品からモダン仕様のものと、魅力に満ちた和食器の世界。でも、種類が多すぎて何をどう使えばいいのか迷うこともありますよね。

私が器使いで心がけているのは、色目の地味な料理には絵柄や型の派手なもの、彩りの派手な料理にはシンプルな器とコントラストをつけること。また、料理を美味しくみせる盛り付け方は、大きめな器を使い余白をたっぷり残すのがポイント。重箱も普段使いで、お菓子やサンドイッチをいれて食卓に出します。料理も器しだいで大変身してしまいます。

テーブルセッティングでは、和風の折敷を洋食に使ったり、高低差のある器の組合せや、ガラス器など質感の違うものを合わせたり、かけ算の妙を楽しんでいます。

Compared to Western tableware, Japanese dishes offer a wide range of variations. In this fascinating world, the shapes and sizes differ, and the material ranges from ceramics to porcelain, or woodenware to lacquerware, spanning traditional crafts to contemporary pieces.

It can seem quite daunting to choose the perfect plate but one of the things I keep in mind is maintaining the contrast between the food and the dishware, like pairing a vibrant dish in an understated bowl. Use large platters with plenty of room to accentuate the dishes, or fill a multi-tiered lacquered box with everyday sandwiches and sweets; the right tableware can transform any ordinary meal into a special experience.

For the table setting, combine platters of different sizes and shapes, lay out Japanese placemats for a Western dinner, or incorporate shiny glassware for a fun twist.

スーパーで買える日本のおみやげ
Japanese Souvenirs Available at the Supermarket

日本のおみやげというと、定番は伝統的なお菓子や和風グッズ。最近は、日本ならではのスナック菓子や食材などが人気になってるそうです。手軽にスーパーなどで手に入るおみやげを紹介します。

Traditional sweets and goods reign supreme as classic Japanese souvenirs, but snacks and food items unique to this country have recently been gaining popularity. Here are some souvenirs you can easily find at the local supermarket.

❶ **Bakauke**
A smile-shaped rice cracker that's soy sauce flavored with a hint of green laver.

❷ **Kaki no Tane**
Crispy seed-shaped rice crackers and peanuts, also known as Kaki-pi.

❸ **Happy Turn**
Individually wrapped crackers sprinkled with savory "happy" powder.

❹ **Instant Miso Soup**
Instant miso soup made from a raw paste combining rice and bean miso.

❺ **Kamameshi no Moto**
Cook rice with this instant mix for delicious and easy gomoku rice.

❻ **Chitara**
A popular finger food made of cheese sandwiched between cod paste.

❼ **Soup Harusame**
Glass noodle instant soup popular for its low calories.

❽ **Kara-age Mix**
Simply coat meat in this mix and fry it to make delicious and juicy kara-age.

❾ **Maruchan Fresh Noodles**
These fresh noodles hardly feel like instant ones and make great ramen.

❿ **Watermelon Gummy**
Soft watermelon-flavored gummies perfect for the heat that are only sold in the summer.

⓫ Tarako Pasta Sauce
Just mix the cod roe sauce with boiled pasta to enjoy this tasty Japanese pasta.

⓬ Furikake
Even without side dishes, you can enjoy bowls of just rice with furikake.

⓭ Hi-Chew
A bestseller for over 30 years, this snack bursts with a distinct fruit flavor.

⓮ Black Thunder
The electrifying taste comes from the exquisite texture of the chocolate cookie and biscuit.

⓯ Mini Yokan
Bite-size yokan with flavors like matcha, chestnut, and red bean paste.

⓰ Jagariko
A stick-shape potato snack with a distinct crunchy texture. Over 100 flavors have been sold.

⓱ Kinoko no Yama
A perfect combo of chocolate and crackers that has been selling for over 50 years.

⓲ Matcha Kit Kat
A worldwide favorite with some variations only available in limited seasons or at local shops.

⓳ Pouch Curry
The best gift for Japanese curry lovers with flavors from local to famous curry shops available.

⓴ Tube Spices
These spice pastes in tubes include raw wasabi, yuzu-kosho (citrus chili paste), and onioroshi (daikon chili paste).

㉑ Dashi Packets
Available in powder form or in small bags, they come in handy when you quickly need to make some dashi.

㉒ Dressing
The shiso and sesame flavors are especially useful for dishes beyond salads.

㉓ Grilled Meat Sauce
Whether marinating or grilling, this sweet sauce adds a burst of flavor to any type of meat.

RECIPES

Tofu Miso Soup
➡p14

Ingredients:
1 package of tofu
1/2 leek
dashi stock:
900 ml water
kelp, cut into 10cm pieces
30 grams bonito flakes
80 grams miso
• See P.125
(How to Make Dashi Stock)

Instructions:
1. Slice the tofu into 2 cm cubes. Cut the leek diagonally into 5 mm slices.
2. Heat up the dashi stock without reaching boiling point. Melt the miso.
3. Add the tofu and leek and heat them up, then turn off the heat.

Japanese Rolled Omelette
➡p18

Ingredients:
5 eggs
5 tbsp dashi stock
3 tbsp sugar
1 tbsp sake
1 tbsp mirin

Instructions:
1. Whisk the egg well, add the seasoning, and mix well.
2. Heat the oil in a tamagoyaki pan (or a round frying pan) and spread evenly. Pour 1/3 of the egg mixture and stir with chopsticks to keep it runny.
3. Pour another 1/3 of the egg mixture and stir gently to gather into half the size of the tamagoyaki pan.
4 Pour the rest of the egg mixture under the omelette to cook and shape the omelette.

Simmered Chicken and Vegetables
➡p22

Ingredients:
4 dried shiitake mushrooms
1 chicken thigh
1 burdock
200 grams carrots
150 grams lotus root
1 konnyaku

Seasoning:
4 tbsp soy sauce
2 tbsp sugar
4 tbsp sake
2 tbsp mirin
2 tbsp oil

Instructions:
1. Soak the dried shiitake mushrooms in water and quarter them.
2. Cut the chicken, burdock, carrots, and lotus root into bite size pieces.
3. Dip the konnyaku in boiling water and cut into bite size pieces.
4. Heat the oil in a pot and sauté the meat, vegetables, and konnyaku together.
5. Once the meat turns white, add the seasoning and 1/2 cup of shiitake stock, cover the lid and simmer over medium heat for about 10 minutes.
6. Remove the lid and simmer until the liquid is gone.

Mixed Rice
➡p25

Ingredients:
3 cups rice

＊All the recipes make 4 servings.
＊In this recipes, numerical value of measuring cup, a tablespoon and a teaspoon are based on the Japanese standards.

2 cups dashi stock, 150 ml can juice of scallops
3 tbsp sake
1 tbsp light soy sauce
1 tsp salt
180 grams canned scallops
100 grams green peas

Instructions:
1. Wash the rice, then add dashi stock, sake, light soy sauce, and salt.
2. Lightly boil the green peas.
3. Add the scallops to 1 and cook the rice.
4. Combine 2 to the freshly cooked rice and mix it all together.

Beef Bowl
➡p31

Ingredients:
150 ml dashi stock
60 ml soy sauce
100 cc mirin
1 onion, thinly sliced
300 grams kiriotoshi (thinly sliced ends of cuts) beef

Instructions:
1. Simmer the dashi stock, soy sauce, and mirin, and add the onion.

2. When 1 softens, add the beef and simmer.

Ginger Pork
➡p40

Ingredients:
4 slices pork loin, thinly sliced
1/2 onion
1 tsp ginger
2 tbsp oil
3 tbsp soy sauce
2 tbsp mirin
2 tbsp sake
1 tsp sugar
1 tbsp vinegar

Garnish:
5 cabbage leaves
8 cherry tomatoes

Instructions:
1. Make small slits in the pork between the fat and meat.
2. Grate half of the onion and thinly slice the rest.
3. Grate the ginger and combine with the grated onion and seasonings to marinate the meat for 15 minutes.
4. Heat the oil in a pan and sauté the sliced onion, then add the meat. Once the

meat looks cooked on the outside, add the sauce and toss around until the meat is coated and the liquid is reduced.

Spagetti Napolitana
➡p40

Ingredients:
400 grams pasta
2 tbsp oil
200 grams onion, cut into 7 mm wedges
8 wiener sausages, diagonally cut into 7 mm strips
5 green peppers, cut into 7 mm pieces
240 grams tomato ketchup
Salt and pepper to taste

Instructions:
1. Boil the pasta. Set aside one cup of pasta cooking water.
2. Heat the oil in a frying pan and sauté the onion. When the onion turns translucent, add the wiener sausages and lastly the green peppers.
3. Add the cooked pasta and tomato ketchup into 2, then mix in the pasta cooking

RECIPES

water and toss well. Salt and pepper to taste.

Mackerel Braised in Miso
➡p44

Ingredients:
4 mackerel fillets
70 grams miso
50 ml sake
1 tbsp soy sauce
3 tbsp sugar
70 ml water
40 grams ginger, thinly sliced
1 green onion, cut into 5 cm pieces

Instructions:
1. Make a cross incision on the mackerel's skin side, then pour hot water over it to remove the smell.
2. In a pot, combine the miso, soy sauce, sugar, water, green onion, and ginger and bring to a boil.
3. Add the mackerel to 2, put an otoshibuta (literally a "drop lid") lid and let it simmer for around 15 minutes.

Chicken Teriyaki with Orange Marmalade
➡p47

Ingredients:
1/2 tbsp oil
3 chicken thighs
A:
5 tbsp marmalade
50 ml sake
100 ml water
65 ml soy sauce
1.5 tbsp sugar

Instructions:
1. Heat the oil in a frying pan and cook the chicken thighs with the skin side down. Flip over when the skin gets crispy, removing oil from the meat with paper towels.
2. Combine ingredients under A to make the sauce.
3. Pour the sauce over the meat in the pan and let it simmer for around 4 minutes. After flipping it over, cook the other side for around 2 minutes.

Sukiyaki
➡p60

Ingredients:
400-500 grams thinly-slice beef for sukiyaki, cut into 6-7cm widths
1 block grilled tofu
200 grams edible-chrysanthemum, cut in half
2 leeks, cut diagonally
200 grams shirataki(yam starch noodles)
8 shiitake mushrooms
2 tsp cooking oil
4 eggs
warishita stock:
3/4 cup soy sauce
3/4 cup mirin
1 cup dashi stock
3 tbsp sugar

Instructions:
1. Boil and cut the shirataki. Slice the tofu into bite-size pieces. Lay out all the ingredients on a large platter.
2. Combine all the ingredients for warishita and heat up the stock.
3. Heat the oil in a sukiyaki pan and lightly cook the meat. Pour in just enough warishita to cover and gradually add in the other ingredients.
4. Crack an egg into each person's bowl and whisk well. Dip the cooked meat and vegetables in the raw egg. Continue to add the ingredients and warishita into the pan as you eat. If it gets too heavily seasoned, adjust the taste with sake or dashi stock.

Rice Cake and Vegetable Soup
➡p75

Ingredients:
4 pieces rice cake
100 grams chicken thigh, cut into 2 cm pieces
4 cups dashi stock
1 tsp salt
1 tsp light soy sauce
4 slices naruto
1 bunch mitsuba
Yuzu for garnish

Instructions:
1. Grill the mochi.
2. Add the salt, light soy sauce, and chicken in the dashi stock and cook until the chicken turns white.
3. In a bowl, add the naruto, mitsuba, and yuzu, then pour in 2.

Deep Fried Tofu Sushi
➡p81

Ingredients:
2 cups rice
4 tbsp vinegar
2 tbsp sugar
Salt to taste
50 grams lotus root, roughly chopped
150 ml water
50 ml vinegar
1 tbsp sugar
10 pieces fried tofu, sliced in half
80 grams sugar
60 ml soy sauce
40 ml dashi stock
2 tbsp sesame oil

Instructions:
1. Cook the rice and combine the vinegar with sugar and salt to make vinegared rice.
2. Simmer the lotus root with water, vinegar, and sugar for about 7 minutes to make vinegared lotus root.
3. Add the vinegared lotus root and sesame to the vinegared rice.
4. Put the fried tofu in cold water and bring it to boil; cook for 20 minutes and drain.
5. Immerse the fried tofu in the simmered sugar, soy sauce, and sake for half a day.
6. Lightly drain the fried tofu and stuff with the vinegared rice.

Red Bean Pancake
➡p108

Ingredients:
Pancakes:
80 grams soft flour
1/2 tsp baking powder
1 egg
60 grams sugar
2 tbsp water
1/2 tbsp honey
1/2 tbsp mirin

Cooking oil
200 grams canned red bean paste

Instructions:
1. Thoroughly sift the flour and baking powder. Whisk the egg and sugar together well. Add in the rest of the ingredients and whisk until smooth. Let the batter sit for 30 minutes.
2. Heat the oil in a frying pan and pour in the batter into approximately 8 cm circles. Cook until the surface of the pancake bubbles up. Flip over and cook for another minute.
3. Combine the second side of two cakes into one cake. Once it cools down, fill it in with red bean paste and pinch to seal the edges together.

本文　B7バルキー・A判・T・46.5kg (0.14mm) ／プロセス4C
カバー　雷鳥コート・四六判・Y・135kg ／プロセス4C ／マットPP
表紙　OKACカード・しろ・四六判・T・177kg ／ DIC N-889
使用書体　こぶりなゴシック・見出しゴ・リュウミンPro・リュウミンStd・Hervetica Neue LT Pro・Minion Pro・Univers・Adobe Garamond Pro
組版アプリケーション　InDesign CC 2017
2019-0103-1.5 (4.5)

山田玲子　Reiko Yamada

クッキングアドヴァイザー

フェリス女学院大学卒。1995年から浜田山の自宅で料理教室「salon de R」を主宰し、家庭料理を中心に、おもてなしのコーディネートを楽しく大胆に伝授する笑いあふれるレッスンが人気。また、男子、父子料理教室などを通じて家庭での食の力の向上を伝えている。「食は一番身近な外交」をモットーに、海外各地で料理教室・イベントを開催し、食の国際交流に力を注いでいる。食品会社のレシピ開発、雑誌、ラジオ番組などでも活躍中。ピアソムリエ、酒エキスパート資格取得。主な著書に「おにぎりレシピ101」（2014／ポット出版）、「NY発！サラダボウルレシピ」（2015／大和書房）など。

Reiko Yamada is a cooking adviser. A graduate of Ferris University, she began teaching cooking in 1995 by hosting workshops, "Salon de R," in her home in Tokyo. Her dynamic workshops that cover topics like home cooking and dinner hosting have built a strong following of students who attend her class for a fun and creative experience. She also actively promotes men's participation in cooking through her lessons.

Championing the idea of food as the most basic form of diplomacy, she hosts workshops at home and abroad as a means of intercultural communication.

She also develops recipes for companies, contributes to magazines and radio programs, and is a certified beer sommelier. Publications include *Everyday Onigiri* (2014) and *Salad Bowl Recipes from NY* (2015).

和ごはん101

2017年11月13日　第一版第一刷　発行
2019年10月 3日　第一版第三刷　発行

著者　山田玲子
構成・文・編集　戸塚貴子
英訳　水野響
カバー・ブックデザイン　小久保由美
写真　難波純子
画像補正　難波純子／四幻社
英文校正　ジョー・フリードマン
カバーモデル　山下 晴／安藤日南
協力　秋田安子
発行　ポット出版
　　　150-0001 東京都渋谷区神宮前2-33-18 #303
　　　電話 03-3478-1774　ファックス 03-3402-5558
　　　ウェブサイト http://www.pot.co.jp/
　　　電子メールアドレス books@pot.co.jp
印刷・製本　シナノ印刷株式会社

978-4-7808-0231-3 C0077
©YAMADA Reiko・NAMBA Junko

※書影の利用はご自由に。写真のみの利用はお問い合わせください。

Wagohan: The ABCs of Japanese Cuisine

by YAMADA Reiko
Writer & Editor: TOTSUKA Takako
Translator: MIZUNO Hibiki
Designer: KOKUBO Yumi
Photographer: NAMBA Junko
Retouch images: NAMBA Junko, Yongensha
English Proofreader: Joe Friedman
Model: YAMASHITA Haru, ANDO Hina
Thanks to: AKITA Yasuko

First published in Tokyo, Japan, Nov. 13, 2017
by Pot Publishing
2-33-18-303 Jingumae, Shibuya-ku Tokyo,
150-0001 JAPAN
http://www.pot.co.jp/
E-Mail: books@pot.co.jp

ISBN 978-4-7808-0231-3 C0077

ポット出版の本　バイリンガルブック101シリーズ　電子書籍も発売中

101人いれば、101通り、好みのおにぎりがあります。マイおにぎりを作ってもらうためのヒントになればと、クッキングアドヴァイザー・山田玲子が101のおにぎりレシピを考えました。全文英訳付き。日本のソウルフード、easy、simple、healthyなおにぎりは海外でも人気です。外国の方へのプレゼントなど、小さな外交がこの本から始まります。

著　山田玲子
希望小売価格／ 1,300円+税
判型／ A5判・並製・オールカラー・126P
ISBN978-4-7808-0204-7 C0077

おにぎりレシピ101

WITH ENGLISH INSTRUCTIONS 英訳付き

EVERYDAY ONIGIRI
101 Healthy, Easy Japanese Riceball Recipes

101 Recipes!
Reiko Yamada's 101 simple and easy riceball (onigiri) recipes include mixed, grilled, sushi-style onigiri and more! This cookbook is a perfect introduction to the art of onigiri-making, filled with unique recipes that are bound to inspire your Japanese culinary creativity. Pick up a copy, and you'll become an onigiri expert in no time!

by Reiko Yamada

●紙版は、全国の書店、オンライン書店、ポット出版のサイトから購入・注文できます。
●電子版はオンライン書店で購入・注文できます。